ENDORSEMENTS

Christ is in us, and therefore we are in God's domain. This domain is broader than a mountaintop, for the Kingdom of Heaven which resides inside us is limitless. The Rock, Jesus Christ was born as a baby, but His influence and power has continued to grow until He has become a huge mountain covering the whole earth. We as believers are called to release the Christ that is within us. We have a personal invitation to demonstrate the glory of the Lord as the water of His Word and Spirit covers the globe. When we, as Paul, learn to enter the realm of the Spirit, to see the revelation of Jesus, our true identities as the Bride of Christ will arise and manifest. Jesus met with Moses face to face, and with Elijah in the still, small voice. Have you ever wondered how Jesus will manifest Himself to you? In *From Heaven to Earth,* my friend and colleague,

Adam Thompson, gives Scriptural insights and the keys to every believer to have a face-to-face, heart-to-heart mountaintop encounter with a real, personal God who desires intimacy with you! This book enlightened and excited my spirit to continue pursuing God with all my heart. The revelation knowledge found in *From Heaven to Earth* will transform your life.

DR. BARBIE L. BREATHITT
Author of *Dream Encounters,*
Gateway to the Seer Realm,
Dream Seer, Dream Interpreter,
and *The A to Z Dream Symbology Dictionary*
www.MyOnar.com (Dream Interpretation Website)
www.BarbieBreathitt.com

Have you ever read a book that excites you to the core as it invites you in deeper encounter with the Lord? Well, *From Heaven to Earth* by Adam Thompson is that book! It is a clear, solid, and powerful work filled with revelation that will ignite your hunger for God. I love this book and I deeply respect and honor its author.

PATRICIA KING
Founder XP Ministries
patriciaking.com

I am so excited about Adam's new book *From Heaven to Earth*. The heart desire of the Father is to fellowship with us in a very real way, manifesting Himself to His people. This timely book gives a wonderful, scriptural foundation for the encounters God wants you to have, empowering your faith to draw near and experience the manifest glory of God.

Adam Thompson is one of the most well-respected prophetic voices in our nation today and I celebrate that God has lead him to write such a timely book. It is time for the Body of Christ to experience new realms of glory!

KATHERINE RUONALA
Author of *Living in the Miraculous: How God's Love is Expressed Through the Supernatural*
Senior leader and founder of
Glory City Churches International
Founder and Facilitator of The Australian
Prophetic Council

If you are like me, you've been frustrated at times, wanting to understand what the Bible means by the types and symbols, even the stories God used. I've even said, "I wish Jesus would just walk through the wall and talk to me, face to face, in regular words I can understand and explain this all to me." Hear me then when I tell you that this book, *From Heaven to Earth* by Adam F. Thompson, is pretty much like that. He opens the Word for you, tells you the stories, explains the symbols, makes it plain, and then, just like you've asked God, Adam applies it to your everyday life! I'm not trying to give him a big head but through his book, Adam becomes almost like Jesus walking through the wall for you! Let him make the new covenant real to you. Allow a personal Jesus to come alive for you through this book. Please accept this—that God has brought this book to you for such a time as this—to make your Christian walk really work for you and to make things so real and so alive—that you find yourself suddenly, almost unexpectedly, walking intimately with God.

STEVE SHULTZ
Founder of The Elijah List website

Adam Thompson's new book, *From Heaven to Earth*, is your exciting invitation to live like Jesus. Too many believers mistakenly think of Jesus' miraculous life as "off limits" to them. After all, He was and is God. This is true. Jesus Christ is our God and our Savior; however, He is also our model for living out what we call "the Christian life." By reading this book, I promise that your understanding of "normal Christianity" is going to be significantly upgraded. Page by page, the longing within your spirit will increase as both the scriptures and stories summon you into the supernatural destiny you were redeemed to live!

What I admire about Adam is that he never compromises in his writing. He never tries to make Christianity something that it was never intended to be by "Amen-ing" some of the more popular trends circulating in the church (which attempt to make the supernatural a side issue). On the contrary, Adam is faithfully calling the Body of Christ *upward*.

Do you want to know the key to breaking out of a boring, humdrum religious rut in your walk with God? I encourage you to start by reading this book, as it will lift your eyes to see what life *in Christ* truly looks like. Get ready to: discover how to truly live "in Christ," how to manifest your Heavenly citizenship on Earth, become Biblically sensitive to the angelic realm, and learn how to drink deep of every supernatural grace and blessing the New Covenant has made available to you!

Has anyone ever told you, "Don't expect to live on the mountaintop with God forever?" This is a deception. Learn how you can continuously experience the mountaintop of God because that mountain actually dwells inside of you!

LARRY SPARKS, MDIV
Equip Culture Ministries
Author of *Breakthrough Faith:*
Living a Life Where Anything is Possible and
co-author of *The Fire That Never Sleeps,*
Columnist, *Charisma Magazine*

This is an excellent book, what a gift to the Church. I believe that this is a crucial book for the Body of Christ and as I read through the pages I felt the Lord is going to bring a greater worldwide corporate shift within His Bride in the area of revelation and understanding their identity and authority in Him as they journey through these pages.

This book is full of rich teaching, deep revelation and insight into what it means to be a spiritual highlander through dreams, visions and divine encounters. I highly recommend this book for anyone seeking to go deeper in Him and receive a greater understanding of the supernatural realm.

This book will position the reader for encounters with Jesus, and fuel the fire and hunger in their hearts to see a deeper revelation of what it means to live out of the glorious truth that we are "seated in heavenly places."

This book has been a huge blessing to me and an honor to read. It is inspiring, scripturally sound and challenging. God has used this book to challenge me to go deeper in Him and I know it will for you too.

LANA VAWSER
Lana Vawser Ministries
www.lanavawser.com

Adam F. Thompson's *From Heaven to Earth* is sure to become one of those go-to books. As a "hard to receive" type, I find it an exciting and non-formulaic explanation of moving in the high places with God, with examples from Adam's own life showing that living as a citizen of heaven is as uncomplicated as meditating on the words of Christ and obeying them. Especially inspirational, are the revelatory keys to release faith to live daily in the realm of our heavenly citizenship. Adam's stand on the confusion in the Church regarding angels and demons is another standout section.

RHONDA POOLEY
Author of *Cambodian Harvest—The authorized biography of Marion Fromm* and *Reverse the Curse of Landmines*

FROM
HEAVEN
TO
EARTH

DESTINY IMAGE BOOKS BY ADAM F. THOMPSON

Divinity Code

The Supernatural Man

FROM HEAVEN TO EARTH

Living Life as a Spiritual Highlander

ADAM F. THOMPSON

DESTINY IMAGE® PUBLISHERS, INC.

P.O. Box 310, Shippensburg, PA 17257-0310

"Promoting Inspired Lives."

This book and all other Destiny Image and Destiny Image Fiction books are available at Christian bookstores and distributors worldwide.

Cover design by Terry Clifton

For more information on foreign distributors, call 717-532-3040.

Reach us on the Internet: www.destinyimage.com.

ISBN 13 TP: 978-0-7684-0804-1

ISBN 13 eBook: 978-0-7684-0805-8

For Worldwide Distribution. Printed in the U.S.A.

1 2 3 4 5 6 7 8 / 19 18 17 16 15

CONTENTS

FOREWORD

God not only wants you to move in dreams and visions, but He has a dream and a vision for your life. He has called you to be a Kingdom influencer. That influence will be unique for each one of us. It may touch nations, churches, your workplace, family, neighbor, or the person you run into on the street. No matter what the scope, each moment of influence advances the heart and Kingdom of God in the earth. I have learned a very powerful truth over the years. In order to move forward in all God has for us, it is vital that we receive a revelation of who we really are. As we go through life, there are many factors that influence our identity, including God, the adversary, people, and natural circumstances. The enemy can have a sense of someone's destiny and work to distort that person's identity in order to keep them limited and bound from achieving the greatness God has for them. Some of the warfare you have experienced in life is not about where you have come from, but where you are going. Spiritual resistance can occur to try to hinder you from advancing into God's fullness. But His Kingdom in you is mighty! When we come into relationship with God, He begins a process in us where He heals, restores, and sets us free from every lie the enemy would use to keep us limited and bound. God's truth and identity begin to prevail in us causing us to walk and live in God's purpose and plan.

That is what Adam F. Thompson's book is all about. He shares deep revelation of who you really are. As you come to know your true identity, all the limits come off your life. You begin to live from the place you were destined to live from. So many get stuck living from this earthly dimension being moved by what they see and feel. They let the natural dictate their lives to them. But in Christ, not only do we receive a brand-new identity, but we also receive a new place to live from. You don't have to live under the same limitations. In fact, you are seated in heavenly places in Christ Jesus and have been blessed with every spiritual blessing in the heavenly realm. God has called you to live from above, not from beneath.

I have experienced this very process in my own life. As God's truth enters into our hearts and minds concerning who we are, a redefining takes place. And this must happen. God will come into your life and begin to define you based on where you are going, not on where you have been. God did this with Gideon. He redefined a man who perceived himself as weak and powerless, and called him a mighty man of valor. This also happened with Jacob. God redefined a deceiver and supplanter as a prince and contender with God. This redefinition removed the limits and set them free to advance in God's destiny for their lives.

As you read *From Heaven to Earth*, you will gain God's redefinition of your identity. You will understand how to live from the heavenly place where you are seated with Christ, far above every lie and work of the enemy. You will increase in supernatural Kingdom influence, and not only will you have dreams and visions, but God will fulfill His dream in and through your life. Get ready to advance and walk in your true heavenly identity!

Matt Sorger
Host of *Power for Life TV*, author of *Power for Life*
mattsorger.com

PROLOGUE

What would you do if you went to sleep one night and awoke to find you are no longer in your bed but in another place out of this world? Would you think you were going crazy, or would you allow the possibility of it being a supernatural event involving God? Once I went to sleep after my evening ritual of reading the Bible and praying, and I awoke to find myself on top of a mountain. Describing this mountain with a human understanding will do it no justice, but in my best effort I will try to describe the splendor and awe I experienced.

I was standing on top of this mountain, it was surrounded by other multicolored mountains; their coloring looked like that of a cup of fruit cocktail. In the valley between the mountains was the most beautiful paradise I had ever seen. The flowers were multicolored, the trees were multicolored—there were trees the colors of the rainbow and then there were trees with colors I have never seen before. It was mesmerizing. I saw myself as an incredible being, as a brother in Christ with the Lord Jesus Christ. The sounds were incredible; there were layers upon layers of harmonies I have not heard before. I was completely filled with life.

When I came back into the natural realm I knew that my life would forever be changed for the better, and it has been. This was just one encounter out of many, and this type of encounter is known as a *mountaintop experience.* Those who have experiences similar to this on a frequent basis are known as *highlanders.* Highlanders are people who dwell in mountains and the higher plains. A highlander can also be a native of the Highlands of Scotland and, in military terms, a member of a Scottish Highland regiment. There are also highlanders in different parts of the world like Mount Hagan in Papua New Guinea.

I am using the terminology of *highlanders* as a parable and a parallel to the people who operate in the spirit realm who live in the higher plains—these highlanders are *you* and me. As Christians with the full revelation of our identity in Christ, we are meant to live out of the knowing that we are seated in heavenly places. I believe that if Jesus was not crucified then He would not have died a natural death but would have walked the earth as a highlander for a long and extended life of hundreds or maybe even thousands of years. Jesus came to earth as God clothed in man's skin, and He was so full of the deity of the Godhead that He was life and full of life. The moment He was crucified at Calvary there was an exchange—our death and mortal life was exchanged for His immortal and supreme life. Our spirit beings are immortal and will live for eternity—either with God in heaven or in hell. Jesus came to give us life, and through the power of the cross, through faith, we are secured with Christ for eternity.

> Highlanders are people who dwell
> in mountains and the higher plains.

As we walk the earth and allow this revelation to expand within us, we will gain a deeper understanding that not only will our spirit man have extreme and eternal life, but that our natural physical body can be permeated with health and a long life too. In Genesis it speaks about man's life being shortened after the fall of man took place, but I believe that this can be reversed through the revelation of the exchange that occurred on the cross and that man can now have a long and fulfilled life. I pray that this revelation will cause you to live as a highlander in the eternal realm.

The word *revelation* should not be used too lightly. It is not just a good concept or an intellectual stimulation; it is something that empowers your life and brings change by allowing you to become sensitive with your spiritual senses and not your natural senses. Your spiritual senses bring you to the position of having an encounter with revelation. Reading and meditating on the Word God can bring illumination to it and transform it to the *rhema* word which brings impartation and communion with God.

Any powerful or supernatural ministry which brings a demonstration of the Kingdom on earth would have experienced revelation with God's Word. Revelation can be compared to conception. A woman conceives, and during the growth of the fetus she may experience some pregnancy discomforts and some pain, but after nine months she gives birth to a baby. In like manner in the spiritual realm, conception occurs at revelation of the illuminated Word, and we go through a period of empowerment (which can cause discomforts) until we give birth to the fruits—the signs and wonders, miracles, and the apostolic manifestations of the Kingdom of Heaven here on earth.

I invite you to take part in this awesome and life-changing experience that is available to every born-again believer. This book will give you a practical understanding and basic teaching techniques to help you live the highlander life.

CHAPTER 1

REVELATION OF JESUS CHRIST LEADS TO MOUNTAINTOP EXPERIENCES

THE KINGDOM OF HEAVEN

When a mountain is seen in a dream or a vision it can be used as a metaphor to depict the Kingdom of Heaven. In both the Old and New Testaments there are references to suggest that mountains are likened to being the Kingdom of Heaven. First, in Daniel 2 we read about King Nebuchadnezzar seeing a statue made up of different elements. This statue was symbolically used to portray the different kingdoms of the earth that bore rulership among the nations and that had influence over the area during that time.

> *This image's head was of fine gold, its chest and arms of silver, its belly and thighs of bronze, its legs of iron, its feet partly of iron and partly of clay. You watched while a stone was cut out without hands, which struck the image on its feet of iron and clay, and broke them in pieces. Then the iron, the clay, the bronze, the silver, and the gold were crushed together, and became like chaff from the summer threshing floors; the wind carried them away so that no trace of them was found. And the stone that struck the image became a great mountain and filled the whole earth* (Daniel 2:32-35).

The stone or rock that came and destroyed the statue symbolized Christ; it became a huge mountain which covered the whole earth, and this mountain was actually the Kingdom of Heaven. *Matthew Henry's Complete Commentary on the Bible* gives a great explanation of how this mountain can be equated to the Kingdom of Heaven:

The stone *cut out without hands* represented the kingdom of Jesus Christ.... This is *the stone cut out of the mountain without hands*, for it should be neither raised nor supported by human power or policy no visible hand should act in the setting of it up, but it should be done invisibly the *Spirit of the Lord of hosts*. This was *the stone which the builders refused*, because it was not cut out by their hands, but it has now become the *head-stone of the corner*. ...It is a kingdom *not of this world*, and yet set up in it it is the kingdom of God among men. The *God of heaven* was to set up this kingdom, to give authority to Christ to execute judgment, to set him as *King upon his holy hill of Zion*, and to bring into obedience to him a willing people. Being set up by the God of heaven, it is often in the *New Testament* called the *kingdom of heaven*, for its original is from above and its tendency is upwards.[1]

Second, in the New Testament we read about Paul being taken up into the third heaven:

It is doubtless not profitable for me to boast. I will come to visions and revelations of the Lord: I know a man in Christ who fourteen years ago—whether in the body I do not know, or whether out of the body I do not know, God knows—such a one was caught up to the third heaven. And I know such a man—whether in the body or out of the body I do not know, God knows— how he was caught up into Paradise and heard inexpressible words, which it is not lawful for a man to utter. Of such a one I will boast; yet of myself I will not boast, except in my infirmities. For though I might desire to boast, I will not be a fool; for I will speak the truth. But I refrain, lest anyone should think of me above what he sees me to be or hears from me (2 Corinthians 12:1-6).

Paul was caught up into the third heaven and the actuality of his true identity in the spirit was shown. He did not meditate upon his weaknesses nor focus on the thorn in his side, but he focused on the supernatural strength of God. He looked toward Jesus who was a supernatural man, but he also saw who he was in Jesus.

Paul was dominated by the man he was in Christ more than by his flesh. Ephesians 2:5-6 says: *"Even when we were dead in trespasses, made us alive together with Christ (by grace you have been saved), and raised us up together, and made us sit together in the heavenly places in Christ Jesus."* Paul realized that he had been raised up and was seated within Christ, and this empowered him and took him into that heavenly place of the "I AM zone." This was a mountaintop experience for Paul. When you study the Word, you will notice that the third heaven is the highest place in heaven—it is a mountaintop experience with Christ.

REVELATION OF JESUS CHRIST

To me the mountaintop experience is the true revelation of Jesus Christ. It is Jesus in His true form as the ruler of all existence. As you go deeper into the layers of who Jesus really is and start to discover who you are in Christ Jesus, your life will be greatly changed. The revelation of Jesus Christ empowers us to hold the keys of the Kingdom of Heaven. In Matthew 16:13-15 we read:

> *When Jesus came into the region of Caesarea Philippi, He asked His disciples, saying, "Who do men say that I, the Son*

*of Man, am?" So they said, "Some say
John the Baptist, some Elijah, and others
Jeremiah or one of the prophets." He said
to them, "But who do you say that I am?"*

Peter stepped forward and answered Jesus. Because of the signs and the wonders he had witnessed, knowing that Jesus moved in power, and experiencing the overflow of Jesus, he could boldly say. *"You are the Christ, the Son of the living God"* (Matt. 16:16). Jesus then answered:

*Blessed are you, Simon Bar-Jonah, for flesh
and blood has not revealed this to you, but
My Father who is in heaven. And I also
say to you that you are Peter, and on this
rock I will build My church, and the gates
of Hades shall not prevail against it. And
I will give you the keys of the kingdom of
heaven, and whatever you bind on earth
will be bound in heaven, and whatever
you loose on earth will be loosed in heaven*
(Matthew 16:17-19).

I believe that Peter only received the full revelation of what he had said once Jesus was raised from the dead. Peter was a rough diamond who had foot-in-mouth disease, who stumbled and had issues, and he even denied Christ three times, but he eventually did receive the keys of heaven when he came to the full realization of who Jesus is.

> The revelation of Jesus Christ
> empowers us to hold the keys
> of the Kingdom of Heaven.

As mentioned above, to partake in mountaintop experiences we need to receive the revelation of who Jesus is and who we are in Jesus. In John 21, we read about the disciples being out on the lake and not catching any fish, when all of a sudden a man appeared on the shore and told them to cast their nets on the right side of the boat. When they did this they caught an abundance of fish, and they then realized that the man on the shore was Jesus. This was the third time that Jesus had revealed Himself to the disciples after He had risen from the dead. Fish symbolically have several meanings, which are dependent upon the context of the dream or image. Fish can represent revelation or can be a metaphor for a believer or for evangelism. When the net was raised, it was full of fish, and it was a sure revelation to the disciples that the man on the shore was Jesus Christ. Once Peter realized this, he dove into the water and swam to Jesus. Jesus had already cooked them breakfast, which consisted of fish and bread, and as the disciples communed with Jesus and ate the fish, they partook in the revelation of Jesus Christ who restored them (including Peter) back to their heavenly positions.

REVELATION LEADS TO CITIZENSHIP

When the Holy Spirit came upon the disciples in Acts 2, Peter gave one of the greatest sermons known to humankind—thousands of people were saved in one fell swoop of the first Gospel spoken. He then finally understood what it was like to live in that eternal realm with Jesus as a heavenly highlander—he had the keys of heaven. Having the keys of heaven enables us to be living testimonies with the power and authority to take dominion on earth as it is in heaven. We are then able to operate out of that eternal realm or the "now faith" realm. I was in a mountaintop experience within my own life when God showed me that there was a deeper revelation of this hidden in a passage of scripture in the book of Acts. This passage tells the story of the apostle Paul who was bound and about to be flogged when he asked the commander, *"Is it lawful for you to scourge a man who is a Roman, and uncondemned?"* (Acts 22:25). In that time period, if you flogged a Roman citizen without permission or without him being tried you would get into a lot of trouble. This question alarmed the Roman official, and in verse 29 it says, *"Then immediately those who were about to examine him withdrew from him; and the commander was also afraid after he found out that he was a Roman, and because he had bound him."* And so the Roman officials backed off.

Paul had a dual citizenship; he was a Roman as well as a Jewish citizen. During that time a Roman citizenship was supreme and above any other citizenship. Paul used his Roman citizenship to save himself. This story can be used as a parable to describe our own citizenship of heaven, as Philippians 3:20 says, *"For our citizenship is in heaven."* God wants us to operate out of this heavenly citizenship, and the Word says that no weapon formed against us shall prosper. When you start to activate this truth by faith and by speaking out, then the principalities will become alarmed, the demons will be terrified, and they will let you go just as Paul was let go by the Roman officials.

> Having the keys of heaven enables
> us to be living testimonies with
> the power and authority to take
> dominion on earth as it is in heaven.

If we do not operate out of our citizenship in heaven then we will start to look to our own self-sufficiency and our inabilities. God doesn't require us to be self-sufficient but to be reliant upon Him. That is why Jesus sent out the 72 men without any money so that they would rely on the sufficiency of God's power: *"Do not take a purse or bag or sandals; and do not greet anyone on the road"* (Luke 10:4 NIV). A purse symbolically means our natural identity; we are meant to see ourselves in Christ, our true identity, and not look to our self-made natural identity. If we fix our eyes upon the author and the finisher of our faith and depend on Jesus Christ, who is also the Alpha and the Omega and the Beginning and the End, and receive the revelation of who He is, then we will realize who we are. Then, by stepping out in faith and our citizenship of heaven, we will be able to have mountaintop experiences within the Kingdom of Heaven.

NOTE

1. Matthew Henry, *Matthew Henry's Complete Commentary on the Whole Bible* (1706), Verses 31-45, section II, 2, http://www.studylight.org/commentaries/mhm/view.cgi ?book=da&chapter=002.

CHAPTER 2

THE DOORWAY OF THE NEW COVENANT

Are you wondering how you can access this mountain-top experience for yourself? You may be feeling as if you are in the dark, or that God is not communicating with you, or you may even believe that you can't hear the voice of God or understand what God is saying to you. In the Old Testament most of the people lived in the dark; they did not know or hear from God and therefore had to receive guidance from the anointed prophets who heard from God. In the book of Numbers it says:

> *Then He said, "Hear now My words: if*
> *there is a prophet among you, I, the Lord,*

make Myself known to him in a vision; I speak to him in a dream. Not so with My servant Moses; he is faithful in all My house. I speak with him face to face, even plainly, and not in dark sayings; and he sees the form of the Lord. Why then were you not afraid to speak against My servant Moses?" (Numbers 12:6-8)

The Lord chose to speak to Moses personally. See, in the Old Testament, only a chosen few of God's people were allowed to be the "go between" or to bridge the gap from humankind to God. They were allowed access to His domain and could converse with God on a one-to-one basis. The High Priest of Israel would be one of those chosen few who would be allowed to enter the Holy of Holies in the temple. He would be relied upon by the nation of Israel to go into the heavenlies and receive Almighty God's will and messages for them and to take the sacrificial lamb before God to atone for the sins of Israel for one more year. But then Jesus Christ, being the rightful High Priest according to His bloodline, sacrificed the perfect and sinless Passover Lamb, Himself, and became the final and eternal Great High Priest. Jesus then charged all believers as His high priests of the temple of God—our own bodies.

As we all carry the fullness of God within us through the blood of the Lamb, we have access to this Holy of Holies. No longer does God only choose a few to enter His domain to represent all of Israel, but now in the New Covenant we are all high priests and all are called to enter into His Holy of Holies to commune directly with Father God.

We are so blessed to be living in the New Covenant. These are exciting times because we now have the ability to see with the eyes of our understanding, our spiritual eyes, as well as have the ability to hear with our spiritual ears. It says in Matthew 13:17, *"For assuredly, I say to you that many prophets and righteous men desired to see what you see, and did not see it, and to hear what you hear, and did not hear it."* God spoke to and revealed Himself to Abraham, Isaac, Jacob, Moses, and Jesus, but now He is speaking and revealing Himself to us as well. This is a wonderful mystery which is spoken about in Colossians:

> *The mystery which has been hidden from ages and from generations, but now has been revealed to His saints. To them God willed to make known what are the riches of the glory of this mystery among the*

Gentiles: which is Christ in you, the hope of glory (Colossians 1:26-27).

Now in the New Covenant we are all high priests and all are called to enter into His Holy of Holies to commune directly with Father God.

In John, Jesus refers to the New Covenant when speaking to the Samaritan woman at the well:

Jesus said to her, "Woman, believe Me, the hour is coming when you will neither on this mountain, nor in Jerusalem, worship the Father. You worship what you do not know; we know what we worship, for salvation is of the Jews. But the hour is coming, and now is, when the true worshipers will worship the Father in spirit and truth; for the Father is seeking such to worship Him. God is Spirit, and those who worship Him must worship in spirit and truth" (John 4:21-24).

Hebrews 10:19-20 says, *"Therefore, brethren, having boldness to enter the Holiest by the blood of Jesus, by a new and living way which He consecrated for us, through the veil, that is, His flesh."* Now is the day when you can just step into that eternal realm with your eyes of understanding and wait upon the Lord. That mountaintop experience is inside of you, and God wants you to operate out of that eternal realm of His heavenly domain. This is the place where the true highlanders exist and live out of their citizenship of Heaven.

THE MOUNT OF TRANSFIGURATION RELEASES FAITH

Christ is in us and therefore we are in God's domain; this domain is a mountaintop which resides inside us. This is like the mountaintop experience where Moses and Elijah met with Jesus. Matthew 17 speaks of Jesus being transfigured on the mountaintop. Many believers read this chapter and assume that only a physical transformation occurred. However, the Lord revealed to me a deeper meaning to this event. I believe that Peter, James, John, and Jesus stepped into another dimension; they crossed over into the eternal realm or the "now faith" realm where they met with Moses and Elijah. When Moses went up to the mountaintop in Exodus 34 and the Lord descended and enveloped him in the cloud, Moses stepped into the eternal realm.

In First Kings 19 when Elijah escaped to the mountain, I believe that he too stepped into the eternal realm. Both of these men in their specified time period on the earth transcended and overrode all natural laws; they superseded the speed of light, time, space, and matter and entered the eternal realm where they met with Jesus in His time period. The time zones from each period of these men's lives amalgamated; they became one in the eternal realm You could even call it the "I AM" zone or the "now faith" zone. I can just picture their meeting—here are five men from different time periods meeting each other for the first time. Moses and Elijah would have asked who the other men were and then, looking to Peter, wondered who he was and how he knew who they were and questioned why he wanted to build three tabernacles.

The mountaintop was the place where the King of Glory revealed His true form; this is the place where real faith is revealed and where the promises are *yes and amen*. I believe that for Moses to understand the law he had to physically meet the fulfilment of the law—the Lord Jesus Christ. In order for Elijah to pass the law to Israel during his time on earth, he too had to meet with the Lord Jesus Christ. The *Matthew Henry Commentary* makes this statement:

Thither the Spirit of the Lord led him, probably beyond his own intention, that he might have communion with God in the same place where Moses had, the law that was given by Moses being revived by him. The angel bade him eat the second time, because of the greatness of the journey that was before him.[1]

Then the law was thus given to Israel, with the appearances of terror first and then with a voice of words; and Elijah being now called to revive that law, especially the first two commandments of it, is here taught how to manage it; he must not only awaken and terrify the people with amazing signs, like the earthquake and fire, but he must endeavour, with a still small voice, to convince and persuade them, and not forsake them when he should be addressing them.[2]

After Jesus met with Moses and Elijah, Moses stepped back into his time period, and that is why his face shone so brightly when he came down from the mountain. Elijah stepped back into his time period feeling renewed and now knowing what had to be accomplished for the New Covenant to come into effect. When Jesus brought the three disciples down from the mountain, He told them, *"Tell the vision to no one until the Son of Man is risen from the dead"* (Matt. 17:9). The disciples had this amazing experience, but they did not understand what had happened. They did not understand this faith realm nor know how to live out of it, and that is why they could not cast the demon out of the boy in Matthew 17:14-21—their experience did not bring an immediate revelation. They received this revelation after Jesus was raised from the dead and they were baptized in the Holy Spirit; this is when the veil was torn and they became supernatural men.

There are so many layers of the revelation of Jesus Christ, the hope of glory that is in us. When we allow that to manifest in our life, He becomes to us the Jesus who is the same yesterday, today, and forever. When we allow that, we bypass *this* timeline and go into a realm of faith, the realm that is eternal, where all the promises are. Jesus *is* the same, yesterday, today, forever (see Heb. 13:8). In other words, He's the past, present, and future all in one. I like to call this bypassing of our timeline, the place of "now faith." It's a different time zone. In fact, there's no time zone in the Kingdom of God. It's an eternal place where all the promises are present for us; where your future, your destiny, is already written. Faith brings that future that's already written by God into the now.

Even the past that God has written is brought into the now. For some of you, the enemy has tried to intercept God's plan for you. There's been trauma. Some of you went bankrupt, were affected financially, were bullied at school, were raped and abused. But we can rewrite our destiny through faith. Faith takes us out of *this* timeline and brings us into the eternal realm, the "now faith" realm, where we don't need to be afraid. Because the Kingdom of Heaven has no time, it's eternal.

In John 6, we read how the disciples were in a boat out on a lake when a storm arose and Jesus walked on the water to them. The disciples were terrified. Just imagine: they're several miles out at sea, there's a storm brewing, it's pitch dark, and someone appears out of nowhere walking on water. You'd freak out, too! They thought it was a ghost. No wonder they were frightened.

The disciples were fearful when they saw Jesus walking towards them, but He is challenging us to allow Him to be in our boat constantly. Sometimes we're double-minded about having Jesus in our lives. God wants us to remain in that place where Jesus is always in the boat; inside me, in my "house."

There's a revelation behind a revelation in this—a story behind the story. Jesus told them, "It is I. Do not be afraid." Only then were they willing to take Him into the boat. And *immediately* they were at their destination on the other shore. That was a supernatural encounter. When we focus on Jesus and meditate on Him day and night, we open a door. There's a door standing open in heaven, but Jesus is also knocking on the door and it will open as we pursue Him, get to know His Word, and allow Him to step into our boat. Some of us need to let Him to do that. You see, the revelation of Jesus Christ is having Him, the hope of glory, *in* us.

Shortly after our church, Field of Dreams, began I developed a major hernia. I could take in only fluids and I couldn't pass anything. I was in hospital on a drip and due to be operated on. I really disliked being in that hospital ward. Using the Gideon Bible, I began searching the scriptures and highlighting the references to healing. As I meditated on the Word I suddenly felt Jesus had stepped into my boat. I felt like the healing was mine, *now*. If we think, "one day I'll be healed" we will always be saying "one day" like the man at the Pool of Bethesda. In that hospital bed it was so real to me that I was healed *now*. So real, that I pulled out the tubes and checked myself out of the hospital. I went home and cancelled the operation. That was in 2007. I have had no hernia problems since. I was completely healed.

You see, faith is like a woman conceiving a child. In the early days she can't see or feel the baby, but it's there. That's the reality. I was conceived with the Word of the Lord that I was healed. I tapped into that zone where Jesus the hope of glory is Christ in me. And when you tap into that reality, nothing is going to get in its way.

Once we acknowledge that we are no longer hindered by an Old Testament covenant and that the door has been opened to us, we can start to communicate with God and partake in our own mountaintop experiences. By taking a step of faith onto the mountain, we will gain our own transfiguration that will activate the "now faith" zone in our own lives. This will open us up to a brand-new world where we become supernatural beings.

NOTES

1. Henry, *Matthew Henry's Complete Commentary* (1706), Verses 1-8, v.8, http://www.biblestudytools .com/commentaries/matthew-henry-complete/1-kings/ 19.html.

2. Ibid., Verses 9-18, v.12.

CHAPTER 3

A BRAND-NEW WORLD

ABIDE IN GOD

To remain in this brand-new world we must understand that under this new covenant we carry God's domain within us—and I don't mean a "kingdomof-heaven.com" domain, but the domain of heaven, the Holy of Holies. That revelation gives us the power and the authority to activate His domain in order to have dominion on earth and self-govern our own lives and govern the Kingdom of Heaven on earth. One of the major keys to knowing God and to having success in living here on earth and to inheriting everything Jesus has, is through the renewing of your mind. When a person receives Christ and is born again, there is a great celebration. That person will usually feel on top of the world or different in a good way. But if people don't want to be discipled or want to grow in God, they will eventually lose their joy and they could easily return to the life and situations they led before their conversion.

It is imperative to have a strong foundational understanding of the Word of God, to be discipled and to renew your mind in order to operate from His domain on earth and in heaven. In the late 1990s, I went through a period in my life where I demanded God reveal His plans and will for my life, and I insisted that Jesus should come and reveal these plans to me personally. In my ignorance I went on a fast; I was determined that Jesus would then appear to me. I would picture in my mind Jesus arriving with an accompaniment of angels, holding the Book of Life in His hands, and He would proceed to read out my destiny—the scene looked like a television show in my head. After many days of not eating I looked terrible and I was approached by my uncle who plainly told me that if I didn't eat I would certainly see Jesus—because I would be dead and in heaven! I was so passionate about knowing my future and knowing

God's will for it, that out of His grace Jesus did appear to me after 28 days of fasting.

Jesus appeared to me like the pictures the Catholics use to depict Him; He was a Jewish man wearing a white and purple robe, His arms were extended toward me, and He just radiated with pure love. All He said to me was, *"Adam, abide in Me."* I snapped out of this encounter, and initially I was very disappointed because I expected Him to sit down with me and to explain everything to me. As I sat at the dining table at 2:30 in the morning breaking my fast, and in between mouthfuls of food, I repeated to myself, *"Abide in me."* I paused and said to God, "Abide in me? I could have just read that! Is that it?" I received no reply. In John 15:7 it says, *"If you abide in Me, and My words abide in you, you will ask what you desire, and it shall be done for you."* A lot of Christians do not understand what it means to abide in Him; it simply means to have His Word written on the tablet of your heart day and night. I listen to His Word day and night, I meditate on the Word, and when it becomes illuminated and brings revelation it enables me to remain in God. Revelation is a key to remaining in God's domain; the Kingdom of Heaven is not upon us but inside of us. It is a place. "Abide in Me" can also mean "dwell in Me."

SENSITIVITY TO THE SPIRIT REALM

By living in this brand-new world we can expect to experience weird and wonderful things. One of the first training events we will experience is the increasing of our sensitivity to the spiritual realm. As Christians, we need to be sensitive to our spirit man and be able to understand what is happening in the heavenlies around us. As I have mentioned in my previous book *The Supernatural Man,* I make use of the term *heavenlies* while some may use the term *second heaven,* but in Ephesians 6 it mentions the word *heavenly places.* There is no scripture verse in the Bible using the term *second heaven.*

> *For we do not wrestle against flesh and blood, but against principalities, against powers, against the rulers of the darkness of this age, against spiritual hosts of wickedness in the heavenly places* (Ephesians 6:12).

Revelation is a key to remaining in God's domain; the Kingdom of Heaven is not upon us but inside of us.

Once we become sensitive to the spirit realm, we are able to discern warnings and uncover the plans of the enemy that could be occurring in that moment or those he is planning for the future. We are actually very sensitive beings; we can be likened to antennas that can pick up frequencies in the spiritual realm, and this is often heightened when fasting and praying. I can only describe us, as being like FM radios. FM radios pick up radio waves in the atmosphere, but in order to broadcast the sound through a receiver, the radio needs to be tuned to the right channel. We need to be tuned in to God.

DREAMS AND VISIONS

I'm using this FM radio analogy to describe a similar principle in the receiving of dreams and visions. Sometimes we don't even realize that we are receiving information from the spiritual realm and are actually experiencing open visions. We as human beings are receiving visions in the heavenlies around us just like the FM radios receive the radio waves, but as we have a different frequency we actually become receivers of visions, open visions, visions of the night, and dreams. Visions and dreams are God's way of communicating with us. God gives us warnings through dreams and visions so that we have a strategy to bind and shut down the plans of the enemy through the blood of Jesus.

I am a man who moves in the prophetic, and I demonstrate the prophetic through dreams and visions. I believe dreams and visions play a very important role when it comes to the gift of operating in the office of the prophet. From experience, I feel that the Body of Christ and many in leadership positions are not ready to receive the realms of dreams and visions as a scriptural and prophetic way of moving in the gifts. Or, they do not recognize that dreams and visions are relevant for today and actually believe that they are dangerous and a form of the occult. This baffles me, as the Bible is full of scriptures about dreams and visions. It was one dream in the book of Matthew 2 which determined the salvation of humankind: *"And having been warned in a dream not to go back to Herod, they returned to their country by another route"* (Matt. 2:12 NIV). The Magi were asked by Herod to return to him and let him know where Jesus had been born so that he too could go and worship Him, but his intention was to kill Jesus. He was oppressed by a demon operating out of jealousy, and he wanted to destroy the child. God gave the Magi a dream, warning them not to go back to Herod. If this dream had not taken place or if the Magi had just merely dismissed the dream, then Jesus would have been murdered and would not have fulfilled His destiny.

> The Bible is full of scriptures
> about dreams and visions.

Angels do speak to us. They are ministering spirits and they speak to us on behalf of the Lord. It happened all through the scriptures. The angels in the spiritual realm work parallel with us in the natural realm. Demons, on the other hand, are sent by satan to torment us. They are very familiar with us and desire not only to torment but also to possess us. As a child of ten or eleven I had a vivid prophetic dream. It was about the technology that was in place to bring back to life people who had been frozen after death. As these people came back to life, it wasn't really them, but familiar spirits who knew those people when they were alive and could imitate them. In my dream these familiar spirits possessed these bodies, denied the Messiah and brought a massive deception that caused even believers to fall away.

There is a great deception coming into the world, and part of that is that people confuse angels with demons, and demons with angels. Demons want to control our lives, angels are sent to help us. But while angels are sent to equip us, they will never inherit what we inherit. They are workers, employees in the Kingdom; *we* are sons in the Kingdom, heirs. Angels will never have that.

John 1 tells us that the Word became flesh in Jesus Christ. The Word is Jesus and angels respond to His command. Angels will always perform God's word. If we meditate on the Word day and night, using our yetza—the redeemed and anointed imagination—and allowing Jesus to be in us, then our destiny in God will be unveiled and made manifest in our lives.

Sadly, I have been accused of being a heretic for teaching on the subject of dreams and visions and for writing the book, *The Divinity Code to Understanding Your Dreams and Visions* with co-author Adrian Beale. When Adrian and I first self-published this book, it contained groundbreaking information that was, at first, not well received by our home country, Australia.

To this day I am still questioned and interrogated by members of the church body. Even though these occurrences are not pleasant, I do understand why believers react the way they do and why there is a hesitancy to accept these teachings as being part of the workings of God. It is correct to say that if a person is not careful and treats this subject foolishly, there is the possibility to operate out of error. It is imperative to always seek out the Holy Spirit's leading with all teachings. But it is undeniable that God does speak to us through the use of dreams and visions; we just need to learn to decode what God is saying. Praise the Lord that things are changing and more people are being receptive to these teachings and our book has since become a bestseller. We are blessed to see people activating the Kingdom of Heaven through dreams and visions through the teaching in our book.

ANGELS IN DREAMS

Usually, in general dreams God speaks to us in riddles and metaphors, but God can reveal angels to us in dreams as well. Some people criticize me because I talk about angels, but it is very important to have angels in your life. It is divination to worship angels; people operating in New Age practices do worship angels, and this is heresy. Some angels are absolutely glorious, but under no circumstances should we worship them. In Revelation 22 the apostle John fell before an angel to worship him and the angel rebuked him:

Now I, John, saw and heard these things. And when I heard and saw, I fell down to worship before the feet of the angel who showed me these things. Then he said to me, "See that you do not do that. For I am your fellow servant, and of your brethren the prophets, and of those who keep the words of this book. Worship God" (Revelation 22:8-9).

Angels were created to serve us; they are the workers in the Kingdom of Heaven. It says in Hebrews 1:14, *"Are they not all ministering spirits sent forth to minister for those who will inherit salvation?"* We have so many angels around us, and a lot of them are feeling quite bored! Yes, you read that correctly, they are bored. They have been sent to assist us, and we don't even acknowledge their presence. There are ministering spirits around us who have been sent to serve the sons of God who are in Christ Jesus and seated in heavenly places with Him. We are heirs to the throne of God, for we are in Christ Jesus and we are seated in heavenly places with Him. The angels want to help us.

A person once came up to me and told me that we had no authority to command angels. In a way that is true; as being merely humans we cannot command angels and tell them what to do. But once we take our natural eyes off the circumstances around us and we praise God, by faith we have access to the courts of heaven as seen in Psalms 100:4:

> *Enter into His gates with thanksgiving, and into His courts with praise. Be thankful to Him, and bless His name.*

When we decree the Word of God, angels will hear and respond to God's Word and take action as stated in Psalms 103:20-21:

> *Bless the Lord, you His angels, who excel in strength, who do His word, heeding the voice of His word. Bless the Lord, all you His hosts, you ministers of His, who do His pleasure.*

We are heirs to the throne of God, for we are in Christ Jesus and we are seated in heavenly places with Him. The angels want to help us.

When a particular person, like a pastor or a mentor in your life, appears in your dreams, depending on the context of the dream that person may represent an angel. If the person is a very prophetic, anointed, and godly person, then he could be representing the Holy Spirit. If he is very Christlike or has the name *Chris* or *Christine,* then that person could be representing Jesus. If the person's name is *Michael,* or he has other good characteristics, he would be representing an angel. You may wonder how people can represent angels. You can read Acts 12, where Peter was freed from prison and went to Mary's house. The disciples didn't believe it was Peter knocking at the door. *"But they said to her, 'You are beside yourself!' Yet she kept insisting that it was so. So they said, 'It is his angel'"* (Acts 12:15). This verse indicates to me that angels can look like us.

A reverse example is that if a person is tormenting you—for example, in a workplace environment—or if a person is nasty, hates you, or has a death wish against you and you have a dream of that person tormenting you, that person may represent a demon which is operating against you. There are no formulas when it comes to dreams; they come in various manifestations, but God can reveal Jesus, the Holy Spirit, and even angels to us through simple metaphors and parables in our dreams.

You can also have encounters in the night where the angel of the Lord may come to you through a dream. This is not a standard dream where God speaks to you in metaphors but is an actual occurrence. This is scriptural, as seen in the book of Matthew: *"But while he thought about these things, behold, an angel of the Lord appeared to him in a dream, saying, 'Joseph, son of David, do not be afraid to take to you Mary your wife, for that which is conceived in her is of the Holy Spirit'"* (Matt. 1:20). This event is called an encounter of the night; I believe this is not a standard dream but a visitation. This type of encounter happened twice to Joseph; the second time the angel of the Lord appeared to him in a dreams, he told Joseph to flee Israel with Mary and Jesus and go to Egypt, for Jesus's life was in danger.

TESTIMONIES OF ANGELS IN DREAMS

I have experienced an encounter of the night before where I had a visitation from the angel of the Lord. One night in 2006, I woke up out of my body. I was walking around the house, and as I looked out one of the windows I saw a company of angels. I was wide awake in my spirit body, but my physical body was still asleep on the bed. There was one angel who was inside the house, and he approached me; he handed me an old leather-bound book. It was beautiful. Engraved on the cover was the word *Resolved*. I opened up the book, and inside was a calendar; the book was actually a diary of 2007 containing some type of hieroglyphics. Due to this encounter, I knew that 2007 would be a significant year and a turning point in my destiny. In 2007, the Field of Dreams church in South Australia was planted, and I went into full-time ministry. This previous encounter with the angel of the Lord gave me the confidence to make the right decisions. Angels in the nighttime is another form of how God can speak to us. I want to encourage you that it is okay to talk about angels; I talk about them all of the time as they play a big part in ministry.

I had an experience where I woke
up but I was out of my body.

I would like to share another testimony. Todd Weatherly and I meet regularly to pray, discuss, and plan for our church, and God has given us great strategies during our prayer time. One time we were praying for finances for our church building, and after our prayer session I had another encounter of the night; I had a visitation from an angel of the Lord. It was quite a dramatic scene as the windows burst open and the drapes billowed around and my spirit man awoke but my body was still asleep on the bed—the scene could easily be compared to a movie. An angel came toward me; he wore a white robe with a gold belt around his waist, carried a sword and had black shoulder-length hair. He said, "I come from the presence of the Lord. This is the word of the Lord; whenever you and Todd get together, whatever you ask for and agree upon, it will be done. Nothing will get in the way of that prayer." It was a very simple statement, but it was so powerful too.

I was so excited to have this experience and hear these words that I had to tell Todd immediately what had happened. Since then we have prayed for quite a lot of things, and it has been so amazing to see God answering our prayers! One of the greatest blessings we had was receiving the finances for our church venue expenses, missions, and evangelistic crusades. We simply prayed and believed God for providing the finances. A few months later someone had even deposited several hundred thousand dollars into our bank account. That is a miracle! We never asked anyone except God for the finances! I just want to encourage you to keep praying in the Holy Spirit and agreeing for the blessings of God for your life, and you will see them manifest.

ANGELS IN VISIONS

I believe that the devil does not own the heavenlies. As our eyes are opened to the spiritual realm and the veil is removed, we are also able to see angels and other heavenly beings. I often see angels, especially when I am ministering in meetings. This seeing is not with the naked eye but is with my spiritual eyes after the veil has been lifted. I trust that you, the reader, are a mature Christian who knows that whatever you receive out of the heavenlies needs to be rightly discerned because demons want to torment you, not serve you. You may have thoughts coming to you in a pornographic, demonic, or lustful nature, and you need to know that these visions might not be coming from within you, especially if you have no issues with these in your life. These images are actually warnings of what is happening around you in the spirit realm. I have received visions similar to this before; I could step into a building or a meeting and pornographic images would just flash in front of me. The Lord has shown me that these are demonic powers in the heavenlies, and these spirits are operating in that particular region. They may be tormenting the person seen in the vision; it may even be the person standing next to you who is being oppressed by them. This is a word of knowledge from the Lord.

> Keep praying in the Holy Spirit
> and agreeing for the blessings
> of God for your life, and you
> will see them manifest.

Out of ignorance, some people—myself included, until the Lord corrected me—will begin to feel guilty for having these thoughts and will often feel condemned. The Lord set me free and released my mind with the revelation that these thoughts and images were things happening in the heavenlies; God is removing the veil and providing us with a strategy to bind the spirits. I was once ministering at a Bible college when I received some images that disturbed me, but as I asked God for more information I realized these visions were words of knowledge. I spoke out the words of knowledge and later two students in the college who were fornicating outside of marriage confessed and repented. Everything is redemptive, it just needs to be done in the right spirit. Those students were restored back to purity.

TESTIMONY OF A VISION

Before I go out ministering, my habit is to lie on my bed and wait on the Lord. I soak in His presence until I go into a trance and receive downloads and visions from the Lord. This is God's way of showing me what is happening around me in the spirit realm.

Once, while I was ministering in South Africa, I stayed in the home of a very wealthy man from the UK. This man had blessed me and the pastor of the church where I was preaching by allowing me the use of his home for a while. The housekeeper took great care of me and prepared all of my meals, cleaned, and tidied the home. So I was lying on my bed waiting on the Lord, I had a horrific vision of this housekeeper being violently raped. This really distressed me. I knew that these visions were not coming from within me, as I have dealt with and been delivered from the lusts of my youth and I have no desire to entertain such thoughts. I spoke to the pastor on the way to the meeting and I told him that we had a problem—that I believed the owner of the house I was staying in was actually raping the young housekeeper. The pastor was shocked and confused and his first response was to tell me that he thought I had the wrong interpretation. I knew that this type of behavior is prevalent in certain regions, so I again stressed that there was a problem and I was quite concerned. He thought I was probably crazy and dismissed it.

The next day I saw this young lady while she was preparing the meals, and I spoke to her and told her what the Lord had shown me. Immediately she started to tear up, and then she broke down in sobs confirming it all. I had the privilege of praying for this young woman and leading her to Christ, and she was born again. The transformation in her face was beautiful as she said the sinner's prayer and accepted Christ—the heaviness just lifted away from her and the house.

In the following days, this young lady was still looking completely transformed and she said, "Brother Adam, I feel so different. I would like you to pray for my sister too." I asked if she would like to bring the sister to the house in which I was staying, but she asked if I would go to their house instead. I stated that I didn't know how I would get to their house as I didn't have transport and that I would have to ask the pastor if he would drive them. Again, I asked her if she could bring her sister to where I was staying. She said the reason she wanted me to come to their home was that their mother was a witch doctor and her sister and herself were being tormented by these creature-like demons which would dance and howl on their rooftop at night. She wanted me to pray for them and set them free from this torment.

I thought to myself, *"Sure, what's a witch doctor! Greater is He that is in me than he that is in the world,"* according to First John 4:4, *"You are of God, little children, and have overcome them, because He who is in you is greater than he who is in the world."* I arranged for the pastor to take me to their home the next day. It was quite an eerie-looking place. I had to walk down a very narrow path surrounded by high grass to get to the house, which was a brick, and tin-roofed shanty built by the government for squatter camps. The atmosphere felt demonic, and there was a real sense of darkness over the area. The mother took off and left for the day because she didn't want to be there. I was very happy about that.

The sisters tried to explain to me what these creatures were that were tormenting them. I asked where they were right now, and was told that they hide in the bushes during the day but they danced and howled on the tin roof at night. This might sound creepy, but this is a reality in some parts of Africa. As I prayed for the sister, she was completely set free straight away and the heaviness over the house lifted off immediately. Again, I wish you could have seen the look on her face—it was completely transformed into light, and she was beaming. She said the sinner's prayer and accepted Jesus as her Lord and Savior. It was a wonderful time, and I praise God for that! Several days later we received a report from the sisters that those demon spirits had stopped tormenting them. I am not sure what happened to the mother, as I believe she was living close by to the girls, but I heard that the girls had joined a church and are going on for God! Hallelujah! What great news!

"You are of God, little children, and have overcome them, because He who is in you is greater than he who is in the world."

When I returned to South Africa some time later, the pastor told me that the owner of the house I was living in had been charged with rape by another lady who was also sexually assaulted by him, and he consequently fled the country. The pastor acknowledged that I had been right in the interpretation of the vision I saw. This just shows that through one step of faith and obedience to a word of knowledge, change can come not only to an individual or a family, but to a whole region.

ACTIVATING DREAMS AND VISIONS

A dream or a vision is a seed which needs to be activated by faith. John 15:16 states, *"You did not choose Me, but I chose you and appointed you that you should go and bear fruit, and that your fruit should remain, that whatever you ask the Father in My name He may give you."* I believe that in this passage of scripture the word *fruit* means "substance" or "faith," and so you can read that sentence as "you may have *faith* to bear *fruit/substance* and then your *faith/fruit* will remain." There are different types of fruit, but through my studies I believe that two of the types of fruit are faith and substance. Hebrews 11:1 says, *"Now faith is the substance of things hoped for, the evidence of things not seen."*

The word *substance* can be substituted for the word *fruit,* which is the evidence or the title deed, of things not seen. If we see with our spiritual eyes and hear with our spiritual ears, the Word becomes illuminated and revelation will activate our faith, which gives us the authority to step out and act upon it. We have five senses in our natural bodies—touch, taste, smell, sight, and sound—but I believe that faith is like a sixth sense. We respond to our natural senses, but we also need to respond to faith as it is the only thing that pleases God: *"And without faith it is impossible to please God, because anyone who comes to him must believe that he exists and that he rewards those who earnestly seek him"* (Heb. 11:6 NIV).

> If we see with our spiritual eyes
> and hear with our spiritual ears,
> the Word becomes illuminated and
> revelation will activate our faith.

We are called to grow as Christians. God didn't save us just to sit on our hands and do nothing; God saved us so that we can bear fruit and fulfill the destiny He has for us. At first Jesus spoke to His disciples in parables and metaphors, but as time progressed He started speaking plainly to them: *"These things I have spoken to you in figurative language; but the time is coming when I will no longer speak to you in figurative language, but I will tell you plainly about the Father"* (John 16:25). The dictionary meaning for *plainly* is "clear to the mind; evident, manifest, or obvious."[1] As believers, I do not feel that it is correct for us to keep relying on those with a prophetic gifting to continuously interpret our dreams and visions for us. If we sit around and discuss our dreams and visions but receive no understanding or revelation about them, then there is indeed cause for concern, as God does not want us to be in the dark and not understand His language. I believe that if people receive the same or similar dreams for years or if they continuously ask others for the interpretation, then they are just being lazy. They do not want to seek out the treasure of heaven but expect it to be handed over to them on a platter. Matthew 7:7-8 states, *"Ask, and it will be given to you; seek, and you will find; knock, and it will be opened to you. For everyone who asks receives, and he who seeks finds, and to him who knocks it will be opened."* What saddens me even more is that a lot of believers will not even do anything with the interpretation once they receive it. Unfortunately, some people in the western world can be quite lazy and have a "quick fix" mentality. I say this bluntly, but it is a reality.

> If dreams and visions are not interpreted they will profit no one.

If you are not seeing God's Word illuminated in your dreams and visions, then there is something amiss. Without reference to the Word of God, it is complete foolishness to continue to discuss the dreams and visions one is having. Dreams and visions are meant to provide revelation to propel believers into their destinies. One can include speaking in tongues in the same principle: *"But now, brethren, if I come to you speaking with tongues, what shall I profit you unless I speak to you either by revelation, by knowledge, by prophesying, or by teaching?"* (1 Cor. 14:6). When Paul, an apostle of the Lord Jesus Christ, taught about tongues, he spoke about the different manifestations of the tongues. For example, when there is an assembly of people there needs to be an interpretation of the tongues spoken. Paul continued to say that if no prophetic word came forth, then those in the assembly and in the surrounding world would think that person would be completely foolish or *"out of their mind."* If speaking in tongues profited no one, then there would be no use for it. In like manner, if dreams and visions are not interpreted, they will profit no one.

SIGNS AND WONDERS

Not only have we been challenged at our church, Field of Dreams, and in our conferences over the teachings of dreams and visions, but also at the signs and wonders that occur in these meetings. Besides the many healings, some people have had oil coming out of their hands, others have had gold dust appear on them, and some have even received gold fillings. People will criticize us and call us "the wicked generation who asks for a sign" (see Matt. 16:4). This would be true if that is all we were doing. If we were only focused on and chasing the signs and not focusing on the One who brings them, the King of Glory, it would be divination and foolishness. Mark 16 says that signs and wonders will follow believers and they will be used to confirm the Word: *"And they went out and preached everywhere, the Lord working with them and confirming the word through the accompanying signs. Amen"* (Mark 16:20). Signs and wonders are an endorsement from God when you preach the Word of God and decree it into existence.

NOTE

1. *Dictionary.com,* s.v. "Plain," definition 2, accessed February 7, 2015, http://dictionary.reference.com/browse/plainly?s=t.

CHAPTER 4

OPERATING OUT OF THE GIFTING AND NOT RELATIONSHIP

There are times when people can move powerfully in signs and wonders but not actually know God. I have been guilty of ministering to people when I have not kept a good relationship with God. As I mentioned in *The Supernatural Man,* I was quite an astute business man in the early 1990s. After I was born again, I entered Bible college and then went into the business world. At this time, my focus shifted from God to work and my relationship with God deteriorated. However, as I have a prophetic gifting, I could use it when I needed to—even when I was not following God—and so I did in my work life.

On one occasion, my newly hired business employee was sitting across from me while I was signing the checks, when I received a word of knowledge through a flash vision of her doing tarot readings. I continued to look down at the checks as I signed them, but I asked her, "So for how long have you been doing tarot readings?"

This question sent shock waves through the heavenlies as her reaction was quite explosive. In anger she shouted, "How dare you judge me! Who do you think you are?" There was so much tension in the atmosphere, but I calmly told her that I was not judging her—I was curious to know the answer. She knew I was a Christian (even though I was not following the Lord at the time) and Christians don't partake in tarot readings.

Due to the gifting in my life I was able to lead this lady to the Lord. After some time, I explained to her the need for baptism in water, but she would always avoid the subject. After a few weeks of my pestering her about this subject, we entered into an argument in front of other employees. She told me that she believed she did not need to be baptized in water, and I tried to explain to her that this was not an option but a commandment. As the argument escalated, the Lord struck her with blindness! When the Lord strikes someone with temporary blindness, the fear of the living Lord quickly comes upon them. It also came upon me as I witnessed this.

We read in Acts 9 about Saul, a persecutor of the disciples of the Lord. He went to Damascus to find both men and women to persecute and was blinded by the Lord for three days until he was baptized by Ananias.

> *And Ananias went his way and entered the house; and laying his hands on him he said, "Brother Saul, the Lord Jesus, who appeared to you on the road as you came, has sent me that you may receive your sight and be filled with the Holy Spirit." Immediately there fell from his eyes something like scales, and he received his sight at once; and he arose and was baptized* (Acts 9:17-18).

In Acts 13, Elymas the sorcerer came against Paul, and Paul rebuked him:

> *"And now, indeed, the hand of the Lord is upon you, and you shall be blind, not*

seeing the sun for a time." And immediately a dark mist fell on him, and he went around seeking someone to lead him by the hand (Acts 13:11).

When the Lord strikes someone with temporary blindness, the fear of the living Lord quickly comes upon them.

These same experiences of temporary blindness had now transpired with my business employee. She hung onto the table and freaked out about not being able to see, so I immediately started to pray for her sight to return. Finally, after ten minutes of fervent prayer, it did return; she decided to be water baptized.

Another event transpired a while later where I operated out of my gifting and not out of my relationship with the Lord. During my years in business, I was also a shareholder of a building company, and we had a teenage girl doing her work experience at our company. She was a very unhappy young lady, her language was foul, and she threw her weight around the office and was quite aggressive to her fellow work mates. This behavior took us all by surprise as work experience students are usually very accommodating and well behaved. One day she was hurling abuse at the photocopier machine; I approached her and asked if we could discuss her behavior and determine what was upsetting her so much. I ushered her into another room and calmly told her that this behavior was not going to help her cause and could easily make the situation far worse. After a while she started to tell me how she was no longer living with her parents; she had left home and was now staying with a friend who was practicing witchcraft. This young girl had been exposed to some occult practices that had scared her greatly. Her behavior was a reaction to the fear that had gripped her life.

I was still not following God a hundred percent at this time. I had backslidden, but out of duty I offered to drive her home at night to ensure her safety to some degree. On the last day of her work experience with us, I drove her home, and on the way I told her that she did not have to live this kind of life. I shared the Gospel of Jesus Christ and how He came to set us free and that He would free her from this bondage of fear. I started quoting the scriptures, *"He who is in you is greater than he who is in the world"* (1 John 4:4), and, *"Behold, I give you the authority to trample on serpents and scorpions, and over all the power of the enemy, and nothing shall by any means hurt you"* (Luke 10:19).

It wasn't my plan to get her saved, but she turned to me and asked me to pray for her right there and then. She said to me, "I want this!" I thought to myself that the timing of all that had transpired was inappropriate. I was lukewarm toward God, and so I told her that there was no appropriate place for me to pray for her. I was hoping that I would just be able to drop her off at home and that at some point in the future she would be able to receive Christ, but she spotted a park and asked me to pull over and said that I could pray for her in the park. I sighed but said okay and pulled over.

We walked to the park bench, and I told her that she would have to say the sinner's prayer, would have to open her heart to Jesus and allow Him to take control of her life, and then she would become born again. I started to pray for her, she repeated the sinner's prayer after me, and then all of a sudden she started shaking and became quite emotional. I had one hand on the top of her head and I continued to pray, but she shook even more and, surprisingly, burst out into speaking in tongues. I was stunned at this occurrence, but then she started speaking even louder. I quickly started to look around to ensure no one could hear her. In shock

I pulled my hand back from her head and looked at it as if it contained some unknown power. I could not understand how this could all be happening, as I was not even following God! We got back into the car and she said she felt different and wanted to know what she should do now that she had received Jesus into her life. So I told her to find and start attending a church and I rattled off a few church names in that area. I finally dropped her off at her home and speedily drove away.

A few years later I rededicated my life to the Lord and I felt as if I was born again—again. My spiritual life and relationship with God was completely revived. God started to pour out His Spirit over me and awesome experiences started to take place in my home. Todd Weatherly came to my home, and we started to pray together. The word spread and people started coming for prayer and left being completely healed after having their own experiences with God. On two separate occasions we had Pentecostal pastors knock at the door. The first time this happened we thought we were in big trouble, as our home meeting was not part of a church—we were independents, so to speak, but on both occasions they just wanted us to pray for them.

One night after we prayed and had our meeting, we decided to go get takeout for dinner. I was waiting for our pizza order to be called when a lady excitedly rushed over to me. She hugged me and said, "It's you! I've been talking about you. Oh my God, it is you!"

I thought to myself, "Who on earth is this woman?"

She must have seen the confusion on my face because she said, "I've been telling all of my friends about you. I am the girl who did work experience at your company. I was the one you prayed for and led to Christ." She continued to say that she was born again and was now a youth leader. I was stunned—five years previously I had just dropped her off at home after I prayed for her, never looked back, and drove away. God had miraculously transformed her life and she was still on fire for Him.

> The word spread and people started coming for prayer and left being completely healed after having their own experiences with God.

The point of these two testimonies is that even though I didn't know God, nor had a good relationship with Him and sometimes had a downright stinking attitude toward Him, I was still able to move in my gifting and experience signs, wonders, and miracles. It says in Romans 11:29, *"For the gifts and the calling of God are irrevocable."* God still used my gifts for His glory, but we are to be careful of how we act on a continuing basis. We are called to have a relationship with God.

> *Not everyone who says to Me, "Lord, Lord," shall enter the kingdom of heaven, but he who does the will of My Father in heaven. Many will say to Me in that day, "Lord, Lord, have we not prophesied in Your name, cast out demons in Your name, and done many wonders in Your name?" And then I will declare to them, "I never knew you; depart from Me, you who practice lawlessness!"* (Matthew 7:21-23)

We were in God's thoughts before He even created us. He knew us before we were born, but I believe God wants us to know Him, have Him in our thoughts, and have an intimate relationship with Him *before* we start to move in creative miracles and our gifting.

Again, signs and wonders come to confirm the Word, but the attribute of knowing God is of the utmost importance. In Psalms we learn that the children of Israel got to see God's acts, but Moses knew His ways: *"He made known His ways to Moses, His acts to the children of Israel"* (Ps. 103:7). The Israelites knew of God, but Moses was intimate with God; God wants us to know His ways and be just as intimate with Him as Moses was.

If you are in ministry or ministering to someone and you move in the supernatural realms, it is imperative to keep the authenticity between you and God. When I was ministering in India, I was moving in the healing realm and I constantly had people knocking at my door at all hours of the day and night wanting prayer for healing. I have a gift, but I knew that if I lost focus on God and didn't retain my intimacy with Him, I would not have been able to carry the weight of ministering to all of those people during the amount of time I had available to me. A gifting brings a "weight" as it operates in power, but if you do not know God or have an intimate relationship with Him this weight will become a burden which will ultimately destroy you.

CHAPTER 5

FISHING IN THE HIGHLANDS

Dreams and visions are a very broad subject, as there are different manifestations and encounters. But, there is one thing that really inspires me about having dreams and visions—it is a wonderful tool for evangelism. A lot of believers don't realize that this is such a powerful tool to win souls. It says in Proverbs 11:30, *"And he who wins souls is wise."* We have to be wise servants and win souls. There is a supernatural element to winning souls; I believe the days of cold-calling people are over. Cold calling can work, although it's less effective nowadays. Having preached on the streets for three years, I could often be found at bus stops preaching to people, and they had to listen to me because they had nowhere to go until the bus arrived. I believe the days of asking people, "Have you found Jesus?" are over. When you ask this question, people look at you as if to say, "Well, I didn't know He was lost?"

I have lead many people to Christ through dream interpretations. I will frequently attend psychic fairs, and people will approach me to have their dreams interpreted. Through my experience, I have realized that a lot of unbelievers will have dreams that point to Jesus. They are often amazed that God is actually speaking to them and is encouraging them to seek Him out. After I have interpreted their dreams, I will step out in faith and say to them, "I am going to pray for you, and while I am praying you will experience an encounter with God." I explain that they might feel warmth or a fire within or a cool breeze across their skin, or it might feel as if an oily substance is being poured over their head. I further explain that they are experiencing the presence of God and the Holy Spirit is revealing Jesus to them. I will boldly say that if they do not feel anything then they are free to call me a false prophet. I know that God will always touch them as their minds have already been opened to the fact that He exists and is talking to them.

After this, I will share a short Gospel message of why Jesus came to earth and how they need to repent of their sins and receive Christ as their Lord and Savior. I then explain further about how God so loved the world that He sent His only Son so that all should not perish but have eternal life. Approximately nine out of ten people will receive Christ and invite Him into their hearts. Some people experience deliverance immediately. We have seen witches, clairvoyants, people operating in the occult, and people from all walks of life being delivered from demons and being totally set free.

> We have seen witches, clairvoyants,
> people operating in the occult,
> and people from all walks of life
> being delivered from demons
> and being totally set free.

Six months ago I ministered at a high school to a group of year 11 students where I had 18 decisions for Christ within two hours. A lot of them are now going on for Christ. One girl was a Buddhist who was powerfully touched by God after she repented and received Christ. She was overcome with tears but was released from bondages and now she will publicly sing and worship the Lord in the school.

WINNING SOULS THROUGH LOVE, NOT FEAR

God wants us to be wise in winning souls; the days of preaching on the street corners are coming to an end, in my opinion. We have witnessed preachers who mean well, in that they want souls for the Kingdom of Heaven, but use tactics of evoking fear and shouting out, "God hates homosexuals!" or "God hates sinners! Repent or burn in hell." Their deliverance of the Word is an example of "How to win friends and influence people—*not!*" I experienced this in one of my first visits to a Pentecostal church in the mid 1980s when my brother invited me to hear an evangelist preach in our hometown. I was a wild fellow in those days, and my intentions were to go to this church to meet some ladies, as I had heard there were some really good-looking girls. This evangelist was preaching hellfire and brimstone, as the saying goes; he was quite intense but was actually quite a good preacher. When he did an altar call I sensed something pulling on my heart. I was feeling emotional, and I could sense the Spirit of God on me. I found myself drawn to the front, and soon I was among 100 other people out of a 3,000-large congregation.

The evangelist had a blond afro with piercing blue eyes, and he stared intensely at people as he was walking up and down the altar. He stopped, and he stared straight at me; he called me up to the platform with an intense voice, "You! You come up here!" I was flabbergasted—out of 3,000 people in the auditorium he picked me to come up to the front. I looked like something the cat dragged in—I had been on a three-day binge, hung over from the night before, and I was wearing a baggy shirt and looking quite unkempt. He looked me up and down and said, "How long have you been living in perversion and sin? Tell everybody!" I was shocked! The auditorium went silent; you could have heard a penny drop. A baby started crying; I looked around the auditorium, and then looked back at him. He said, "Come here, I'm going to pray for you." He put his hands on me and he tried to cast out a spirit of lust from within me. He shouted out, "Lust, come out!" and he was pushing my head intensely, and he kept on pushing down onto it. My eyes were staring out at the 3,000-strong crowd, and I was completely humiliated. After everyone said the sinner's prayer, we were directed through a side door for further ministry, but because of my extreme feelings of embarrassment I walked straight through the crowd and back to my seat.

I tried to deny and push the event out of my mind as it seemed so unreal. I was feeling so humiliated, but I tried to ignore that fact. I looked around me and there was an array of empty seats; the group of young ladies who were sitting with us earlier had left. Not only did my plan of meeting ladies and trying to hook up with them fail, but now I was humiliated too. I remember when I went back home after this ordeal, my brother approached me and said, "Hmmm, that was great, I think."

I asked, "What do you mean that was great? I feel like my life has been flushed down the toilet!" I stormed off to bed, and as I replayed the events of the night I became more humiliated, which started to turn into anger.

As time went on, I became even angrier at what had happened. Every time someone mentioned they were a Christian I would see red and almost go into convulsions. I was anti the whole Christian scene, because I was publicly humiliated. Six months later I was out to a very wild party. I was drunk, and at one point I sensed danger and thought a fight would break out soon, so I decided to leave the party with my good friend John Pedder. I was so drunk that I was actually seeing double. We climbed into the car and through my intoxicated overconfidence, I decided to drive us home.

It was a cold night, and I was trying to clean the window, as it was foggy, when all of a sudden I heard a huge bang. I had driven under a truck! Thank God that my friend and I were not harmed—I could have killed both of us that night. This experience tormented me for a few days. The owner of the truck called the police, as he sensed I was intoxicated. When the police arrived on the scene, I realized how badly it looked and I thought that this was the end of me—I'd surely be put away and be in serious trouble with the law. I moved away from the scene slightly and I started praying. John asked me what I was doing and I told him that I was praying; I was going to ask God to get me out of this situation. I bargained with God and told Him that if He got me out of this situation I would go back to that stupid church and make a decision to follow Him.

The police came over to me with a breathalyzer to test how high my alcohol consumption was. I was so nervous, but I tried to act sober, even though I was still seeing double of everything. The police officer went under the street lamp to record the reading of the breathalyzer; he came back and told me that I was clear to go—there was a negative reading on the device. To me, this was a miracle! I took it as a sign that God was watching over me while I was drunk. I went back to the church the following weekend and repented. I gave my heart to the Lord and became born again, and I went full steam ahead for God.

Three months later, my friend John, who was in the car with me, also received Christ as his Lord and Savior and became born again through witnessing the transformation God had made in my life. To this day John continues ministering in our church and has the power of a prophetic gifting.

It is my conviction that in order to win souls to Christ we need to communicate the love of God and build relationships with people. Jesus built a relationship with the woman at the well. He moved in a supernatural element of knowing that she had five husbands—this word of knowledge opened up her heart to receive that He was a prophet. After further conversation, she received the revelation that this prophet was indeed the Son of God, Jesus Christ. What amazes me is that she instantly became an evangelist and went through her town telling everyone to come and meet Jesus:

The woman then left her waterpot, went her way into the city, and said to the men, "Come, see a Man who told me all things that I ever did. Could this be the Christ?" Then they went out of the city and came to Him (John 4:28-30).

Revival broke out in this city. This woman had issues and was rejected by her people, but through the love of Jesus forming a relationship and conversing with her when no one else would, she was set free and became an evangelist and led her city to Christ.

In order to win souls to Christ we need to communicate the love of God and build relationships with people.

As I mentioned before, we need to be wise in winning souls, and dream interpretation is a great method for leading people to Christ. You can also move in words of knowledge as an evangelist by receiving visions or getting downloads from open visions. Open visions can come through fasting and praying in the Holy Spirit; my book, *The Supernatural Man,* explains this process in more detail. I often get downloads and words of knowledge, and sometimes while I am on the street I will receive open visions. I will then go out and minister, speaking out the words of knowledge and prophesying into people's lives, which can cause them to open their hearts to receive Christ. Again, like the woman at the well, Jesus knew she had five husbands, and through the words of knowledge she opened up to receive from Jesus and thus perceived that He was a prophet. She was open to receiving ministry from Jesus.

CHAPTER 6

HIGHLANDERS IN ACTION

I once heard a friend talk about mountains, and he mentioned that mountains are a place inside of us where the time of eternity leads to mountaintop experiences with Christ. The Kingdom of Heaven is inside and upon us, and what empowers us to have the Kingdom of Heaven cross-pollinate onto the earth is the revelation of Mark 11:23: *"For assuredly, I say to you, whoever says to this mountain, 'Be removed and be cast into the sea,' and does not doubt in his heart, but believes that those things he says will be done, he will have whatever he says."*

There are many layers of revelation to Mark 11:23—the mountain could mean a literal mountain or it could be used as a metaphor to describe problems. A Christian businessman named R.G. LeTourneau had this scripture in his heart when he invented the excavator. An excavator literally moves mountains. The other layer of revelation is that the mountain can mean the Kingdom of Heaven. Through revelation of being in that place, caught up with the Lord and seeing and hearing with our spiritual eyes and ears, it unveils eternal substance for us to act upon. This empowers us with a God-faith, not human positive thinking, which will move mountains and the Kingdom of Heaven into the sea. The sea can be a metaphor for humanity or the world.

I believe that this passage of scripture shows us that we can move the Kingdom of Heaven by faith for it to be manifested on the earth or cast into the earth to establish a reformation with signs and wonders. I am convinced that in this age believers will come into such an understanding of this truth, and it is my revelation that through these revivalists and reformers, the shaking of the community will stir up and cause them to become a living testimony according to the prophecy spoken in Malachi 4:6:

And he will turn the hearts of the fathers to the children, and the hearts of the children to their fathers, lest I come and strike the earth with a curse.

I believe that God is changing the mindsets of believers so that they move out of religion and start to walk in this eternal realm.

HIGHLANDERS IN BUSINESS

You may have heard the phrase "kings and priests" being used by Christian men's groups at business seminars. The "kings" are a representation of the businessman while "priests" represents the pastor or persons in ministry. For years, ministers have depended upon the businessmen to finance them and their ministries, and this has become a mindset that needs to be changed. Now is the era where God is raising up ministers who are entrepreneurs operating a cash cow. Kathie Walters has spoken about cash cows in her meetings; a cash cow is when a person receives creative ideas from God to start a business that will generate an income for their ministry:

When they had come to Capernaum, those who received the temple tax came to Peter and said, "Does your Teacher not pay the temple tax?"

He said, "Yes."

And when he had come into the house, Jesus anticipated him, saying, "What do you think, Simon? From whom do the kings of the earth take customs or taxes, from their sons or from strangers?"

Peter said to Him, "From strangers."

Jesus said to him, "Then the sons are free. Nevertheless, lest we offend them, go to the sea, cast in a hook, and take the fish that comes up first. And when you have opened its mouth, you will find a piece of money; take that and give it to them for Me and you" (Matthew 17:24-27).

If you just read the above scripture at face value you will notice that God performed an amazing miracle—He made money come out of a fish! If you delve in deeper, there is another dimension to this scripture passage; as mentioned before, there are different types of metaphors for fish. It can be a believer, evangelism, or revelation. In this section of scripture, Jesus is encouraging Simon to pursue the heavenly blessings of the Kingdom of God. The water is a metaphor for the gifts of the Spirit, the line is the encouragement to pursue God, the fish is a metaphor for revelation, and the coin can be a metaphor for financial provision. This is the revelation of Jesus Christ—who He is and who we are in Him—and this will help us tap into the ingenious mind of God which will bring provision for the Kingdom of God and ministry.

> A cash cow is when a person
> receives creative ideas from God to
> start a business that will generate
> an income for their ministry.

I mentioned R.G. LeTourneau at the beginning of this chapter:

> A sixth grade dropout, Robert Gilmore "RG" LeTourneau went on to become the leading earth moving machinery manufacturer of his day with plants on 4 continents, more than 300 patents to his name and major contributions to road construction and heavy equipment that forever changed the world. Most importantly, his

contribution to the advancement of the Gospel ranks him among the greatest of Christian Businessmen of all time. Famous for living on 10% of his income and giving 90% to the spread of the Gospel, LeTourneau exemplified what a Christian businessman should be.[1]

He had incredible, inventive ideas—the excavators, the electric wheel, tree lobbing equipment, the cart that pulls the planes, and offshore oil riggers. These were just some of his ideas. He also established universities, Christian camps, training centers for missionaries, and flew worldwide to preach to churches and Christian entrepreneurs. His goal was always to bring God into the community. R.G. was a man who operated out of mountaintop experiences and made a considerable impact, not only on his local community but on the worldwide community too. He is not the only Christian businessman to do this.

TESTIMONY OF A MODERN DAY "AVERAGE MAN"

This is the testimony of my friend Rick, who came from a very messed-up life as a drug addict and heroin dealer before meeting Jesus and being born again. During the early years of being a Christian, he got into a religious rut, but God came to the rescue by giving him dreams that lead him to Adrian Beale and myself for interpretation. This began a friendship where we could minister to him, and he was able to renew his mind, learn about the spirit realm, and activate the revelations he was receiving by stepping out in faith and doing what God had called him to do.

> At a very early age I began to take drugs, which led me to have a nervous breakdown, and thereafter I also developed cancer. After being diagnosed with cancer, I decided that I wasn't going to be around much longer, so I started to take drugs in a greater measure. I smuggled drugs from Mexico to Hawaii on a 38-foot ketch, I smuggled heroin out of Panama, I did four years of jail time, and I was in mental institutions. One day I found myself sitting on a rock in Bondi; I had just written suicide notes—one to my mother and one to my friend who I had just ripped off by $10,000.00 through drug deals, I was shooting up five grams of heroin a day, and

it was not even touching the sides. I turned to a guy who was with me and I said to him, "I have had it!" and then I said these three fateful words, *"God help me!"* And God stepped in and performed the miraculous. Within 24 hours I was on a train heading to Canberra. I got off the train, caught a bus, and as I got off the bus I saw my mother and the first thing I said to her was that I was going to go into detox, and that is where my life with God began.

One day a nurse in the Alcoholics Anonymous center made a simple statement: "Most people who end up in the hospital are sick," and that was when I saw God written all over the walls in that room. I knew then that God was the only one who could help me through this experience and through life. It took me two years of rehabilitation to get my head straight, but in these two years of sorting my life out I lost my mother (I had lost my father when I was in jail), I lost my aunty a year after my mother died, and then I lost my grandfather—I lost my whole family within two years of being sober, but not once did I pick up a drink during this time, thanks to God.

I decided to go to a church, and I listened to a Baptist minister by the name of Bob Payne preach the Gospel. I sat in that seat shaking like a leaf. I couldn't wait any longer for an altar call, and so I just ran to the front and gave my heart to the Lord. Thereafter I joined a Charismatic church, and this is where I met Adrian Beale.

During this time, I had a screen printing business that was tied up with some people, and I ended up going bankrupt. I started questioning about what was going on as I was going to church, I was tithing, I was doing everything I thought I had to do, but now I had to go and get a real job—so I worked in the mud and the dirt as a pipe layer. One day I received a phone call from a friend named Marie. She told me that Adrian Beale had written a book with Adam Thompson (I didn't know who Adam was then). She was telling me that this book was about dreams, and I told her that I don't even have dreams, but she gave me a copy of the book anyway. So I started reading *The Divinity Code,* and all of a sudden I had a dream. I thought that was strange, so I rang up Adrian and made contact with him again, and he introduced me to Adam who interpreted the dream.

I started to get more dreams, and I learned how to interpret them. Then all of a sudden things didn't seem well at work (on the outside it all seemed fine but there was something wrong and I couldn't put my finger on it). I received a vision—it was a basic vision of me leaving my house and my wife and there was a porcelain toilet. In the natural you would think that if I did that—leave my house and wife—I would end up in the toilet, but the way God was talking to me He was saying that I needed to leave the church, get rid of the way I do things, and find a place to detox. I had more dreams after this where God showed me the condition of the church, and then He told me to leave my job—that was a hard thing to do because in the natural everything looked fine. I left my job and started working with two other men, and we worked for a builder. I started questioning again—here I am a Christian and Jesus said that He came to give me life abundantly but I didn't have an abundant life. I felt ripped off; things just never seemed to be going right.

Thereafter I had a mountaintop experience with God, He took me to a barren region; it was like nothing I have ever seen on earth. The whole landscape was gray, and there was no color to be seen anywhere. I, however, was dressed in a white T-shirt and a white pair of jeans. The air felt heavy and like a vast void. God showed me this and said that this is what my life had become—my life was now barren and there was no fruit even though I was a Christian. God started dealing with me and the sin in my life through more dreams, and all I could do was just believe that God was in this with me. I, however, needed some friends to stand by me, and I called upon Adrian and Adam to help me.

The person I was working with told me that he was leaving his job and asked me to join him in a new venture; I was finally in the right place at the right time with the right people. We bought an old backhoe for $20,000.00. We worked on it for 90 days, and during this whole time I kept receiving dreams. These dreams required that I now had to believe what God was showing me, that I had to learn to understand this spirit realm and walk by faith. I started applying everything that God was revealing to me, and I started to renew my mind. In the natural, things just seemed not to add up, but I continued to walk by faith. At times I would find myself on my knees repenting, praying, and crying out. God continued to take me down this path of unchartered territory, and I just kept walking and believing.

We bought another excavator and then another one, and now, four years later, we have five 30-ton excavators, twenty men working for us, two Bobcats, a fleet of cars, lots of other equipment, and we are building a whole township. We are involved in the whole infrastructure. Now we are bringing in over a half a million dollar turnover every month. God is doing an incredible thing in my life, and His blessings keep growing. The more I walk in the things of God, the more I am starting to understand that God wants the best for me. I don't know how far this will go, but I do know that there is no other path I will take than the one I am on, as this is the one God has destined for me to walk in. I am so grateful for my God, my Jesus, my Holy Spirit, and my life!

I have been able to use the money God has blessed me with to help other ministries. Currently I am an agent for Ana Mendez Ferrell from the Voice of the Light Ministries, which is now being established in Australia. I believe this is a major part of what God wants to establish in this nation, and what God is about to do on this earth is big and beyond our wildest dreams. I have dedicated my life to God for 21 years now. I rely on our mountaintop experiences, the dreams, and the visions He shares with me; the spirit realm has become more real to me than this natural realm, and all I can say to encourage you, the reader, is that if God can turn my life around and use me—a normal person— then He can do it for anybody. It is just a matter of stepping out and following the God we serve.

Rick came out of the darkness into the light. He was completely transformed, and his life bears much fruit. He has financially sown into the Kingdom quite generously and brings the Gospel of God wherever he goes. He is a great example of renewing one's mind, being open to the revelation brought through dreams, visions, and mountaintop experiences. By just stepping out in faith, it can bring so much change to the world we live in.

Are you called to be a Christian businessman or entrepreneur? Tap into this revelation of Jesus Christ and pursue God, and He will give you inventive downloads that will support you and your ministry. I pray that any holds the enemy has on your finances will be instantly broken as you read this book. I pray for supernatural downloads from heaven to permeate your mind and to be released through your business life. I speak greater intimacy between you and Jesus, and as you eat the fish with Him there will be full provision for your life and ministry.

NOTE

1. RG LeTourneau: Earthmoving Innovator," Giants for God, accessed February 08, 2015, http://www .giantsforgod.com/rg-letourneau/.

CHAPTER 7

HIGHLANDERS KNOW THEIR IDENTITY

God is calling the Body of Christ to rise up in the knowledge of the Kingdom, to tap into the incorruptible seed of Christ, and to live in the highland area as a true highlander. This lifestyle will bring about much revelation that will place you above world systems, giving you influence over councils, governments, and even nations. I want to encourage all believers that this lifestyle is not only for a select few, but is available to everyone in the Body of Christ.

I was a school dropout, and if God can call me to the nations, then He can call anybody to the nations.

I am by no means an elite person. God is calling His entire army to rise up—that includes you—to partake in the highlander lifestyle. The crux of living as a highlander is to be in constant communion with God out of the realms of heavenly places through an intimate relationship with Him. Before an intimate relationship can be truly solidified, it is important for believers to understand who they are in Christ. Unfortunately quite a few believers do not know how special and important they are to God and what it means to be a son of God.

Teaching one about their identity starts from a very young age. Have you noticed that if a child is labeled as naughty and troublesome, they tend to live up to that label? They are constantly behaving in troublesome ways, but if you turn that around and label them as being kind and good they strive to meet those expectations. The same is true for believers—if you teach a believer that they are righteous in God's eyes and focus on how God sees them, then they will live out of that knowledge and eventually, over time, not believe the lies of the enemy that they are less than worthy of God's love and blessings.

The Spirit of God is in all of us and is the essence of who we are. The Kingdom of God is in us, but unless we have a strong, focused, and renewed mind we might not amount to anything. God wants us to have dominion over our lives. In Colossians it says that we came out of the domain of darkness and into sonship of the Kingdom. The key to fulfilling the destiny of God placed within us and allowing us to reign from above and not beneath, is having a strong, focused, and renewed mind. Teaching these truths about identity to believers can begin at any age.

> Quite a few believers do not know how special and important they are to God and what it means to be a son of God.

When my daughter, Savannah, started school, we were all so excited about this new chapter in her life. One day the teacher called us in for a meeting and gave us less than welcoming news—my daughter had been diagnosed with dyslexia. Initially I was shattered and grieved over this diagnosis, as I too had dyslexia and I knew all too well the difficulties that lay ahead, not only with the academic side of things but socially too. In my case, I found that people focused on the problem and not my strengths. This led me to believe that I was inferior and worthless. Ultimately, the only way I could deal with the emotional turmoil I was in was to drop out of school.

I told the teacher not to tell my daughter about the diagnosis. We proceeded to focus on her strengths; we made sure that we spoke life into the situation and declared the word of God over her life. We never focused on the negatives but always decreed the promises of God for her life, and we discipled her by how God saw her. She knew her identity and that she was seated in heavenly places, and she lived her life from the knowledge that she is from above and not from below. In John 3, John the Baptist says that those who are from above are above all—we all have been raised up with Christ and are seated with Him in heavenly places. We all are able to live from this place and not allow our circumstances to dictate how we should be living.

I am so excited to see how much Savannah has grown and how she has blossomed over the years. She is now about to finish year 12 as an A-grade student, and is the school captain. All of this could only have been accomplished with a strong focused mind, a belief in the promises of what God has for her, and by teaching her who she is in the Kingdom.

CHAPTER 8

THE FOUR STAGES TO MATURING AS A HIGHLANDER

As I mentioned in Chapter 7, it is important for a believer to know their identity in Christ as this will bring a deeper understanding and appreciation of having mountaintop experiences. I also want to stress that mountaintop experiences can look different for various believers—for me and those mentioned in this book, they have been through dreams and visions. These encounters with the supernatural realm have kept us returning to the mountaintop until we reached a stage of maturity where we now dwell like the highlanders and live in constant communion with the Lord.

There have been four distinct stages that I had to go through before I reached this place of maturity to operate in the prophetic ministry. These might not be the stages that you will experience, but they are used as an example of how I have learned to dwell on the mountaintop.

STAGE 1: DISCIPLINE AND SELF-GOVERNANCE

It says in Hebrews that God spoke to our forefathers through the prophets, but in these last days God speaks to us by Jesus (see Heb. 1:1-2). Every believer can hear the voice of God, and Jesus Himself said that *"My sheep hear My voice"* (John 10:27) and if we are followers of Jesus then we can hear His voice. Before I could start impacting the Kingdom, I had to learn to identify the voice of God. The easiest way to test if a voice is the Lord's is to obey what you believe He has spoken. God spoke to me directly about my life before He shared about anyone else's life with me. Both Adrian and I can testify that when we started with dream interpretations, the dreams we received at first were about us and our lives individually.

God speaks to us first in order to teach us to be disciplined and able to self-govern our lives. Jesus said, *"First remove the plank from your own eye, and then you will see clearly to remove the speck from your brother's eye"* (Matt. 7:5). God's discipline is not about us keeping the law of the Old Covenant and, should we somehow break just one of the laws, then we have broken them all and have to suffer God's punishments. God can never be upset or disappointed by us if we walk by the Spirit and by faith.

> *There is therefore now no condemnation to those who are in Christ Jesus, who do not walk according to the flesh, but according to the Spirit. For the law of the Spirit of life in Christ Jesus has made me free from the law of sin and death* (Romans 8:1-2).

God's discipline is one of love and gentle guidance, and He does this because He does not want us to step into the arena of operating in the Kingdom only to self-sabotage our lives and not live the life He wants to bless us with.

God spoke to me directly about
my life before He shared about
anyone else's life with me.

When Paul wrote to Timothy, he said:

*Likewise deacons must be reverent, not
double-tongued, not given to much wine,
not greedy for money, holding the mystery
of the faith with a pure conscience. But
let these also first be tested; then let them
serve as deacons, being found blameless.
Likewise, their wives must be reverent,
not slanderers, temperate, faithful in all
things. Let deacons be the husbands of one
wife, ruling their children and their own
houses well. For those who have served
well as deacons obtain for themselves a
good standing and great boldness in the
faith which is in Christ Jesus* (1 Timothy
3:8-13).

We are to manage our lives and have them in order;
an internal success will always come before an external

success. God wants us to be successful and to mature in Him.

Let's use great sporting athletes and their ability to self-govern as an illustration. From a purely physical perspective, they train very hard to reach their sporting goals. They are disciplined in that they eat correctly, train daily, and persevere in all that they do. Their entire focus is on building their physical strength and stamina. If this focus does not extend to the rest of their lives—to their relationships and to their spiritual growth—they will often find themselves falling down from their podiums. Their lives self-destruct, and more often than not they destroy the lives of those closest to them as well.

> An internal success will always
> come before an external success.
> God wants us to be successful
> and to mature in Him.

One of the ways that God often brings correction in my life is through my wife's dreams, funnily enough (who says that God doesn't have a sense of humor?). As an example, one night my wife dreamed that I was approached by a ten-year-old boy who asked me to buy him cigarettes, as he was under age. In the natural there is no way I would even have had a thought to do such a thing. As soon as my wife told me about the dream, I received the interpretation of this parable via the Spirit. Cigarettes can be a metaphor for an offense, and I was in the thicket of offensive situations.

There are two guarantees in this life when you operate in the role of a pastor or the prophetic—some will hate you and some will love you. At times I tended to come home and offload my grievances and annoyances to my wife. I did not realize that my children were overhearing my complaints, and over time they started to take on the offense of the people I spoke about. As one knows, offense is the biggest hindrance to the growth of the church and Body of Christ.

Through the interpretation of this dream, I knew that I had to not only stop speaking negatively about people in front of my children, but to shut down all negativity as it was causing my family to stumble and falter in their spiritual growth. I repented immediately, and the spirit of offense was neutralized and couldn't attack my family any longer.

STAGE 2: GAINING INFLUENCE IN THE LOCAL CHURCH

As you start to manage and expand from the walls of your own temple and grow in a disciplined life, God starts allowing you to influence the Body of Christ through ministering in the local church. This influence starts to develop our prophetic gifting and creates a governmental role from which we can operate. This stage can be lengthy, and I find that a few believers see this time as very testing and frustrating. Some often complain that their pastors do not recognize their prophetic gifting or that their pastor does not pursue the gifts and experiences of the Spirit, and they wish to leave the church and go rogue. Unless God says otherwise, you don't need permission to leave a church; you can use your own initiative to move on, but I encourage you to seek and join other like-minded people who are moving in the Spirit. At the end of the day, God wants all of us to be among people who share the same DNA spiritually, and where there is unity, blessings will flow. In the book of Acts, everyone came together and were of one mind, *"When the Day of Pentecost had fully come, they were all with one accord in one place"* (Acts 2:1), and through this unity they experienced a massive outpouring of the Holy Spirit; this birthed the new covenant era of the church.

The local church is one of the best places to mature, not only as a Christian but as a highlander. Don't expect your pastor to recognize your gifting overnight. We are all growing from glory to glory, but as you remain faithful and obedient to the will of God, the pastor will start to see the favor of God upon your life and you will be given more opportunities to share and minister with others. In saying this, it is not about man's approval, but God will make a way through the anointed gifts on your life: *"A man's gift makes room for him, and brings him before great men"* (Prov. 18:16).

I do have a concern when it comes to believers who have a prophetic gifting and do not want to establish themselves in a church but instead go off as self-proclaimed prophets. They prematurely leave a church to travel from one church to another to disrupt meetings by giving prophetic words in a grand display of self-importance. These prophetic words are often referred to as *car park prophecies,* and I call these people spiritual butterflies—they never settle down and allow themselves to be held accountable for the words they have spoken.

Relationships have to come first, before prophetic ministry. Daniel was a great prophet; he had a great friendship with those around him and worked on strengthening his relationship with King Nebuchadnezzar. Out of this relationship he earned respect, and this allowed him to be a voice among the people. The same principle applies within the Body of Christ—one needs to build a relationship with the leaders of the church. If you continually bring words to the pastor or the leadership and they still don't recognize your gifting or act upon the words, it is okay—don't let this stop you from sharing what God is telling you. I believe that if you are faithful in small things, then God will put you in charge of greater things. Again I say, it's not about being recognized by man or corporate ladder climbing, but it is about building relationships and being recognized by God as a good and faithful servant. The anointing brings the gift and the gift makes the way for a man, and eventually God will take you from glory to glory and your gifting will be noticed and respected.

I found personally that one of the best ways for me to grow in my gifting and to understand and love people was through my pastoral role (I am a prophet, but I also hold the position of a pastor). Being an itinerant minister and travelling to various churches around the world, I am a lot more sensitive to the needs of a pastor and his church as I have the knowledge of how a church functions. My aim is always to leave a good seed to be nurtured and not to leave the church in a spiritual mess.

> Relationships have to come first,
> before prophetic ministry.

When I first started growing in my gifting, I helped my local pastor by interpreting dreams and visions for couples. On one particular occasion I was doing pre-marriage ministering to a couple when one night I had a dream that they should not get married and I told them so. Sometimes when you release a word through a dream interpretation, people do the opposite of that word, and in this instance the couple were led by their emotions and not by the Spirit and so they got married.

While they were away on their honeymoon, I had an intense and vivid vision in the night of this lady. She was sitting on the edge of my bed, and as she turned to look at me I saw that she had a black eye. When I came out of the vision, I was left feeling extremely concerned about her safety. On impulse, I phoned her the next day to see if she was alright. I told her about the vision I'd had, and she was quite emotional on the other end of the line; she said a few words and then hung up on me. I thought that her reaction was quite strange, and I wondered if I had done the right thing by contacting her. That night I received a very harsh phone call from her irate husband who rebuked me for my behavior. He said that if I had any concerns I should have gone to the pastor and the elders of the church first and not have phoned his wife on their honeymoon. He was completely right, of course; I should have contacted the pastor first.

The next thing I knew, I was summoned to the church. The pastor was not happy with my behavior at all. He challenged me on my interpretation of the vision, and then he grilled me on my attitude. I felt like a poodle stuck in a thunderstorm; I was so scared about the ramifications of my actions. The jury was still out on my prophetic gifting, and now my ministry was in jeopardy. Three weeks later, the husband of this lady did indeed beat her up, kicked her out of the house, and changed the locks. I was 100 percent right in the interpretation of the vision, but the delivery of that message and the wisdom to bring a solution to the problem was 100 percent incorrect.

If you don't have a close relationship with God and you don't know the heart of the Father, it won't matter how gifted or how accurate you are in the prophetic—this gift will become a curse. Without an intimacy with God, your gift will come across as a cheap party trick, which can land you in a lot of trouble. These days I am more like an iceberg in that you will only see the tip of me—I keep the downloads and prophetic interpretations of dreams and visions inside of me, and I take them to the wise counsel of the Lord and only release them when the Lord tells me to.

I also learned not to let these mistakes hold me back. It is a guarantee that all of us will make mistakes along our journey, and if you do make a mistake, do not believe that makes you a false prophet. I have discovered that false prophets can be very accurate with their words. They can receive amazing revelations, but they will put the church and the Bride down and start to isolate people from the church to gather them unto themselves. God does not want us to set ourselves up as idols but as icons. An icon is a person or thing admired and regarded as a symbol of a way of life or set of beliefs. We are meant to be shining icons representing Jesus.

> If you don't have a close relationship
> with God and you don't know
> the heart of the Father, it won't
> matter how gifted or how accurate
> you are in the prophetic—this
> gift will become a curse.

After a period of continuous growth and never believing that the mistakes made me worthless, I started to hit the bull's-eye on the interpretations I released, and this earned me respect from my pastor. My father, who is a well-respected man in our community, was the founder of Crime Stoppers in South Australia and received a medal from the Queen of England making him a representative of the Queen. He taught me from a young age that respect cannot be bought or demanded but has to be earned through trust. Trust comes from believing the Word of God and obeying the guidance of the Lord.

May I suggest that you offer to relieve your pastor from various jobs and take on some pastoral care for yourself? The experience is so beneficial in that not only will you learn to love people, but you will learn the mechanics involved in running a church and you will have a greater understanding and sympathy for all of the issues a pastor has to deal with on a daily basis. The pastor will also appreciate the help.

At our church, Field of Dreams in South Australia, we encourage and mentor those willing to grow in the gifts of God. We do move in the prophetic and support those with a prophetic voice. We have found that as we forge strong relationships with our fellowship, our church has been saved from various spirits and demonic attacks wanting to tear our church apart. Our watchmen (prophetic voices) have been able to forewarn us and protect the Bride of Christ. As we all work together to equip the five-fold ministry, we are also preserving and nurturing the Bride, bringing her into a place of complete beauty.

After your time of serving the local church, God will start to expand your area of influence and allow you to impact the universal Church. Here you will be able to influence and encourage others operating in the same gifting as you do. I thoroughly enjoy meeting new ministries and partnering with them to equip the Body of Christ. I never tire of learning from other ministers, sharing testimonies, and having a joyful time with my brothers and sisters in Christ. We truly allow each part of the Body of Christ to supply their gifts to advance the Kingdom of God.

STAGE 3: INFLUENCING THE MARKETPLACE

After some time God moved me from the walls of the church and positioned me in the marketplace. I was now entering the third stage of my prophetic growth. Influencing the marketplace comes with various levels of evangelism. As I have mentioned previously, I love to minister at psychic fairs, and I have led many people to Christ through dream interpretations at these fairs. When God places us among non-believers, He requires us to be wise as serpents yet gentle as doves. We are meant to be wise in our ministering by building rapport and relationships with people, but at all times the love of Jesus needs to be evident.

Dream interpretation has been one of the best ways to evangelize to people, as they are hungry to have their dreams interpreted. Generally speaking, non-believers' dreams mostly point to their need for Jesus. Once I was privileged to lead over 150 people to Christ in only one day in my hometown. I give God all of the glory, as I could never have done that in my own strength. Dream interpretations do not only happen at psychic fairs. I have also led many school students to the Lord.

> When God places us among non-believers, He requires us to be wise as serpents yet gentle as doves.

God also wants us to evangelize and touch business-people. Once I was ministering in Hong Kong, when a group took me out for dinner and asked me to minister to some corporate employees. The next thing I knew, I was in a board meeting held by a prestigious bank. I felt out of my league—I was dressed casually while everyone else was suited, as they were quite renowned and prolific in their industry. My uneasiness quickly turned into satisfaction; I was enjoying interpreting their dreams, and they were so receptive to the interpretations. I was ministering to a very heavy-set man when tears started to form in his eyes; he told me that when he was a child growing up in China he was told that there was no God. He had always believed that there was a God, but no one would confirm it for him. It was a momentous occasion for me when I led this man to Christ; the joy was unspeakable.

The favor of God can really open up when you take the time to minister to businesspeople. God so greatly wants us to tap into the ingenious mind of Christ to speak with wisdom and provide solutions to business and corporate problems. In Genesis 41, when Joseph interpreted Pharaoh's dream he received his freedom, but the word of wisdom or the revelatory knowledge that was over Joseph's life gave him the solution to the problem the Pharaoh was experiencing. In so doing, he was given control to lead the whole nation of Egypt.

I truly believe that this type of wisdom is available to the whole Body of Christ. As we grow in maturity and the knowledge of the glory, we will have the full understanding of the realities in the Kingdom of Heaven. Jesus says that unless we become like little children, we will not see the Kingdom of God: *"Assuredly, I say to you, unless you are converted and become as little children, you will by no means enter the kingdom of heaven"* (Matt. 18:3). He wants us to rewire our minds, humble ourselves to His teachings, meditate on the promises of God, and build a new framework based on the supernatural and spiritual realities of the Kingdom of God. We need to declare these promises over our lives and over the lives we are meant to influence. In Job 22:28 it says, *"You will also declare a thing, and it will be established for you; so light will shine on your ways."*

Children up until the age of five naturally operate out of their spiritual understanding, and it is only through human conditioning that they learn to live in this humanistic world. In essence, we are to become like five-year-olds again from a spiritual perspective. Most children under the age of five believe what they are told and utterly trust their parents. We are to utterly trust God and believe that we can operate in His Kingdom and allow it to manifest here on earth.

> He wants us to rewire our minds, humble ourselves to His teachings, meditate on the promises of God, and build a new framework based on the supernatural and spiritual realities of the Kingdom of God.

STAGE 4: INFLUENCING NATIONS

The fourth stage God has brought me to is influencing the nations and governmental agencies. I currently have my training wheels on in this stage. I have thoroughly enjoyed ministering all over the world and impacting the church and the marketplace. Now, I am excited about impacting the nations. In the next chapter, I will testify as to how I am impacting the nation of Papua New Guinea; for now I want to focus on equipping you to influence nations.

All of the teachings that are currently being released and the stages that one has to go through, are part and parcel of preparing for the second coming of Christ. The Body of Christ is being equipped and matured through Kingdom connections and through the truth that we are now from the incorruptible seed line of Christ. This incorruptible seed line is coming from the order of Melchizedek, according to the Letter to the Hebrews; Jesus Christ is identified as *"a priest forever according to the order of Melchizedek"* (Heb. 7:17). This seed line is from Abraham, Isaac, Jacob, Moses, David, Jesus, and now us. Jewish people understand that they are from the seed line of Abraham and have lived their lives from this knowledge. They know what it means to meditate on God's Word day and night and to believe the promises God spoke in the Old Testament.

One of the reasons why they wear the *kippah* on their heads is to show that they honor God. They have truly believed God's Word, and so they have been able to experience wealth that is above the world's system of wealth. Some of the wealthiest families in the world are Jewish. Unfortunately, a few of them have missed the entire truth of Jesus Christ and do not know that He too is part of this incorruptible seed line, but I believe God is restoring that belief among His people.

> The Body of Christ is being equipped and matured through Kingdom connections and through the truth that we are now from the incorruptible seed line of Christ.

There are some great scriptures that the Jews have adhered to and that are beneficial for the Body of Christ today. The first is Deuteronomy 28:1-14:

> *Now it shall come to pass, if you diligently obey the voice of the Lord your God, to observe carefully all His commandments which I command you today, that the Lord your God will set you high above all nations of the earth. And all these blessings shall come upon you and overtake you, because you obey the voice of the Lord your God:*

Blessed shall you be in the city, and blessed shall you be in the country. Blessed shall be the fruit of your body, the produce of your ground and the increase of your herds, the increase of your cattle and the offspring of your flocks. Blessed shall be your basket and your kneading bowl. Blessed shall you be when you come in, and blessed shall you be when you go out. The Lord will cause your enemies who rise against you to be defeated before your face; they shall come out against you one way and flee before you seven ways. The Lord will command the blessing on you in your storehouses and in all to which you set your hand, and He will bless you in the land which the Lord your God is giving you. The Lord will establish you as a holy people to Himself, just as He has sworn to you, if you keep the commandments of the Lord your God and walk in His ways. Then all peoples of the earth shall see that you are called by the name of the Lord, and they shall be afraid of you. And the Lord will grant you plenty of goods, in the fruit of your body, in the increase of your livestock, and in the produce of your ground, in the land of which the Lord swore to your fathers to give you. The Lord will open to you His good treasure, the heavens, to give the rain to your land in its season, and to bless all the work of your hand. You shall lend to many nations, but you shall not borrow. And the Lord will make you the head and not the tail; you shall be above only, and not be beneath, if you heed the commandments of the Lord your God, which I command you today, and are careful to observe them. So you shall not turn aside from any of the words which I command you this day, to the right or the left, to go after other gods to serve them.

Genesis 12:1-3 is another favored scripture:

"Now the Lord had said to Abram: Get out of your country, from your family and from your father's house, to a land that I will show you. I will make you a great nation; I will bless you and make your name great; and you shall be a blessing. I

will bless those who bless you, and I will curse him who curses you; and in you all the families of the earth shall be blessed.

In Genesis 27, the incorruptible seed of God is revealed through Isaac blessing his son Jacob:

So Jacob went over and kissed him. And when Isaac caught the smell of his clothes, he was finally convinced, and he blessed his son. He said, "Ah! The smell of my son is like the smell of the outdoors, which the Lord has blessed! 'From the dew of heaven and the richness of the earth, may God always give you abundant harvests of grain and bountiful new wine. May many nations become your servants, and may they bow down to you. May you be the master over your brothers, and may your mother's sons bow down to you. All who curse you will be cursed, and all who bless you will be blessed'" (Genesis 27:27-29 NLT).

It seemed to be the other way around for Esau. He was the man of the flesh, he sold his birthright to Jacob, and he was greatly grieved when he learned that

Jacob had received his blessing from Isaac. He begged Isaac to bless him too. His blessing is:

Then Isaac his father answered, Your [blessing and] dwelling shall all come from the fruitfulness of the earth and from the dew of the heavens above; by your sword you shall live and serve your brother. But [the time shall come] when you will grow restive and break loose, and you shall tear his yoke from off your neck (Genesis 27:39-40 AMP).

Unfortunately, in today's society there are many Christian businessmen and women who operate out of the flesh. I don't know how many times I have heard someone say, "One day, when I have earned all of the money I am working toward, then I will sow into the Kingdom." They are working by the sweat of the brow and they are getting smashed by the enemy as they are bowing down to the system of this world and not to the system of heaven. God wants the Body of Christ to tap into this incorruptible seed where we will get the dew of heaven first, then the riches of the earth, and then the nations will bow down to you. Before a worldwide revival breaks out, I believe that the Bride of Christ needs to have influence over the nations.

CHAPTER 9

INHABITING THE HIGHLANDS

CHANGING A NATION

A few years ago I had a mountaintop experience with the Lord where I received a vision for the nation of Papua New Guinea. I spoke out this prophetic word for Papua New Guinea to my coordinator for that country, Alice McCann. In the vision I saw a firewall surrounding Papua New Guinea. This firewall was protecting the country from Islamic extremists and terrorists. I saw missionaries who came to this country and plowed the hard ground and sowed many seeds. I saw a huge harvest coming in. The minerals of the earth, like gold, were rising up out of the ground; the nation was coming into such a blessing filled with riches and opulence. The nations of Malaysia, Philippines, Indonesia, Solomon Islands, Fiji, Australia, and America were in awe of the blessings pouring out over Papua New Guinea. The favor of God was evident all over this nation.

This reminded me of the days when King Solomon was ruling in Israel and the Lord's favor and blessing manifested over the nation. People both within the country and its surrounding neighbors admired the great testimony of God's goodness over that nation. Prior to the blessings being poured out over Israel, the Lord came to King Solomon and said:

> *If My people who are called by My name will humble themselves, and pray and seek My face, and turn from their wicked ways, then I will hear from heaven, and will forgive their sin and heal their land* (2 Chronicles 7:14).

I saw Papua New Guinea as a parallel of Israel; once the people humbled themselves and repented, God would heal their land and pour out His blessings over their nation. In the vision, God gave the nation of Papua New Guinea a new name, and it was, "The Nation of God's Favor."

> People both within the country and its surrounding neighbors admired the great testimony of God's goodness over the nation.

The prophetic word that accompanied the vision was that God was not looking for any heroes, as the ground had already been plowed. He was looking for spiritual fathers. The scripture of Malachi 4:6 came to my spirit during this word:

> *And he will turn the hearts of the fathers to the children, and the hearts of the children to their fathers, lest I come and strike the earth with a curse.*

When a reformation comes to a country, it is important to have spiritual fathers available to equip another generation to flow in a continuous revival state so that the blessings can sustain the nation.

Since I released this word a few years ago, I found out that Papua New Guinea has an annual national day of repentance on the 26th of August. Repentance Day was established on August 15, 2011 by Prime Minister Peter O'Neill and was announced eleven days prior to the first Repentance Day celebration.

> Prayer ceremonies were held in churches throughout the country. In Port Moresby, the capital, a ceremony at the Rev Sioni Kami Memorial church was attended by "representatives of 20 provinces" and various "national leaders" and "church leaders," for "special prayer and Bible readings" and "thanksgiving prayers." Participants asked God to lead the nation. A parish priest in Boroko was reported by *The National* as saying that religious values were "essential to our identity and our culture," and people's church attendance on such a public holiday revealed a difference between Papua New Guinean identity and that of many other countries. On Karanget Island in Madang, the day was celebrated through children depositing the national flag on a church altar, symbolically "deliver[ing] the nation to God."[1]

> The Israelites understood that an act
> of repentance is a spiritual law—once
> obeyed, the blessings of God will flow.

I have heard that since Repentance Day initially started the nation has changed its constitution, they have torn down their idols, businesses are starting to emerge and grow, and the country is starting to experience great blessings and is beginning to prosper. God cannot be mocked, and so He has ensured that corruption is being exposed and the government is finally dealing with the issues instead of sweeping them under the carpet. God is truly building up this nation, and it's all because they took it upon themselves to believe God's Word—that if the people of a nation will truly humble themselves and repent, then God will heal their land and bless it. The Israelites understood that an act of repentance is a spiritual law—once obeyed, the blessings of God will flow. This spiritual law will apply to any nation in today's age; the proof is evident in the nation of Papua New Guinea. I believe that Papua New Guinea will be a forerunner for all of the nations in seeking God and receiving His blessings. I also saw one very bright star shining in the Southern Cross in the vision I had, and I believe that the shining star is Papua New Guinea.

I held on to the vision I had while dwelling in the mountaintops, and finally this year I was able to witness its revealing from the heavenlies into the earth. I was invited to Papua New Guinea to participate in the national Repentance Day by some pastors. These pastors are advisors to the government, and so it was a great honor to have been invited. I was asked to release a word for the nation over the radio, but before I could I had to release the word to the government officials at Parliament House. I brought a film crew with me into Parliament House to record the message I would be releasing over the nation. As I released the word, the officials looked at me alarmed and they shut down our meeting. Afterward, I had no idea what I had done wrong to cause such an alarming reaction. Even the camera man commented that the officials were looking at me as if they were terrified. I was discouraged and believed that I had somehow landed myself in hot water.

Some cross-cultural and miscommunication issues arose from this and caused some confusion. It took some time before I received the explanation of the officials' reactions. Unbeknownst to me, as I was releasing the word I exposed some classified information; I mentioned that they would be changing the name of the nation. I said that the name would be changed to "Favor" as the current name, *Papua New Guinea*, is a cursed name. This new name was actually one of the options that the government was considering using. After having lunch with the Prime Minister and governmental officials, we had the opportunity to discuss the word I released to them, and they gave me permission to release it nationally. I was able to go on the government radio, which airs to 2 million listeners, and I released the Word of God for this blessed nation.

I believe that none of this could have been possible if it had not been for the churches of that nation pursuing God with diligence. I would like to honor a good friend of mine, Joseph Kingal, who was one of the heroes of that nation. He was a great evangelist who plowed the hard ground and received hundreds of thousands of decisions for Christ over the years. When he passed away, they held four state funerals for him. He too was a highlander; he dwelt with God, and through his mountaintop experiences a whole chain of events started to evolve and the harvest is still continuing to come in. Being a highlander is such a privilege as you can create positive changes wherever you go.

BEING A HIGHLANDER IS IN YOUR DESTINY

The Lord knows that my heart is for His people. I want to see them walk in their full destiny as children of the Most High God. During the writing of this book, I had another mountaintop experience with the Lord, and the message that came forth was for you, the readers—my brothers and sisters in Christ. I believe that each and every one of you will be playing a major role in revealing Christ to the nations in these last days.

It felt like I was woken up from my sleep only to find myself in a vision having an encounter with the Angel of the Lord. It reminded me of Zechariah being awoken from a deep sleep by an angel in Zechariah 4:1-2: *"Now the angel who talked with me came back and wakened me, as a man who is wakened out of his sleep. And he said to me, 'What do you see?'"* I saw a very ugly man standing in front of me. He had massive ears that were about half the length of his body, and his face was hideous. Even in the vision, I wondered who this ugly man was. My thoughts were distracted by a beautiful melody that seemed to increase in volume as it came closer to me. The ears of this ugly man slowly changed into wings, and they began to flap faster and faster.

The man's face started to morph, and he became quite handsome. Suddenly he just flew away.

I was confused as to what had just happened, but the beautiful melody lingered and caught my attention again. I turned around, and I saw this stunning angel singing. I cannot begin to describe the sound that came out of his mouth; it was definitely out of this world. The angel was singing in an unknown language, but at the same time it sounded as if an orchestra were playing the most beautiful symphony that I have ever heard. Even the sound waves were not natural—they can only be described as supernatural sound waves that bounded toward me and completely enveloped me. I could feel the glory of God surrounding me. My whole essence was being changed by the presence of God.

Alice McCann was asleep in the adjoining room, and the melody coming from the angel actually woke her up from her sleep. The next day, Alice asked me why I was playing such beautiful music in the early hours of the morning when everyone else was asleep. She was surprised when I mentioned that it was actually an angel playing heavenly music. She felt disappointed that she had gone back to sleep instead of staying awake to listen to the heavenly music.

I could feel the glory of God
surrounding me. My whole
essence was being changed
by the presence of God.

I believe that this angel was a prophetic angel that has come in these critical times to let us know that God is raising up His prophetic voices in this hour. I also believe that this is the same type of angel Jesus sent to John the apostle on the island of Patmos in Revelation 1 to release revelation to equip the Body of Christ for the end times. Now is the time for the Body of Christ to come up the mountain and to dwell there as highlanders. Only then can we operate out of that place with Kingdom knowledge and release those manifestations to the people who are yet to be saved and delivered here on earth. Are you ready to step into your destiny? Your destiny can be found in Jesus Christ our Lord. We are hidden in Him and He is in us as stated in Colossians 1:27: *"Christ in you, the hope of glory."* We are the true highlanders.

NOTE

1. "Repentance Day," Wikipedia, accessed February 09, 2015, http://en.wikipedia.org/wiki/Repentance_Day.

ABOUT ADAM F. THOMPSON

Adam F. Thompson has a remarkable grace to interpret dreams, move in the Word of knowledge, and demonstrate the prophetic. Supernatural signs and manifestations regularly accompany his ministry as he desires to see Jesus magnified through the moving of the Holy Spirit. He has ministered extensively in North America, New Zealand, Korea, and Australia. He also has spent the last fifteen years doing mission work throughout Pakistan, India, Africa, Indonesia, Papua New Guinea, Malaysia, and the Philippines in crusades, feeding programs, and pastors' conferences. Adam is instrumental in planting Field of Dreams church in South Australia and is the author of the *The Supernatural Man* and co-author of the bestselling book *The Divinity Code to Understanding Your Dreams and Visions* and operates itinerantly through his ministry, Voice of Fire.

www.voiceoffireministries.org

www.thedivinitycode.org

www.fieldofdreams.org.au

Made in United States
North Haven, CT
13 November 2022

26678629R00088